God, philosophy, universities

God, philosophy, universities

A Selective History of the Catholic Philosophical Tradition

Alasdair MacIntyre

A SHEED & WARD BOOK

ROWMAN & LITTLEFIELD PUBLISHERS, INC.
Lanham • Boulder • New York • Toronto • Plymouth, UK

A Sheed & Ward Book

ROWMAN & LITTLEFIELD PUBLISHERS, INC.

Published in the United States of America
by Rowman & Littlefield Publishers, Inc.
A wholly owned subsidary of The Rowman & Littlefield Publishing Group, Inc.
4501 Forbes Boulevard, Suite 200, Lanham, Maryland 20706
www.rowmanlittlefield.com

Estover Road
Plymouth PL6 7PY
United Kingdom

British Library Cataloguing in Publication Information Available

Library of Congress Cataloging-in-Publication Data:

MacIntyre, Alasdair C.
  God, philosophy, universities: a selective history of the Catholic philosophical
tradition / Alasdair MacIntyre.
    p. cm.
  Includes bibliographical references and index.
  ISBN 978-0-7425-4429-1 (cloth : alk. paper) — ISBN 978-0-7425-6549-4 (electronic)
  1. Catholic Church and philosophy—History. 2. Philosophy—Study and teaching—
History. 3. Universities and colleges—Curricula—History. 4. Catholic universities and
colleges—Curricula—History. I. Title.
  BX1795.P47M325 2009
  190—dc22   2008048468

Printed in the United States of America

∞ ™ The paper used in this publication meets the minimum requirements of
American National Standard for Information Sciences—Permanence of Paper
for Printed Library Materials, ANSI/NISO Z39.48-1992.

~

Contents

~

Introduction

Three convictions led to the writing of this book. The first is that an educated Catholic laity needs to understand a good deal more about Catholic philosophical thought than it now does. The warring partisans on the great issues that engage our culture and politics presuppose, even when they do not recognize it, the truth of some philosophical theses and the falsity of others. If we are to evaluate their claims, we had better know something about philosophy and, if we are Catholic Christians by faith and commitment, something about Catholic philosophy.

A second underlying conviction is that Catholic philosophy is best understood historically, as a continuing conversation through centuries, in which we turn and return to dialogue with the most important voices from our past, in order to carry forward that conversation in our own time. So we only know how to direct our enquiries now, if we have first made our own the philosophical thought of our predecessors. A third conviction is that philosophy is not just a matter of propositions affirmed or denied and of arguments advanced and critically evaluated, but of philosophers in particular social and cultural situations interacting with each other in their affirmations and denials, in their argumentative wrangling, so that the social forms and institutionalizations of their interactions are important and none more so than those university settings that have shaped philosophical conversation, both to its benefit and to its detriment.

I hope to find readers for this book among undergraduates in their senior year, first-year graduate students, the teachers of such undergraduate and

1

graduate students, and more widely in the educated reading public. It is not a book written for scholars and academic specialists, but of course it invites and will receive their criticisms. I hope that I have made no mistakes of fact, but experience suggests that I should not be too optimistic. There will certainly be quarrels about my principles of selection, about what I have emphasized, and what I have omitted. There will be those who want a larger place for Scotus or Suarez, those who find this book too Thomistic, and those who do not find it Thomistic enough. It is generally plain, I think, which arguments I endorse and which conclusions I reject and on many issues there will inevitably be numerous dissenters, Catholic and non-Catholic.

Since 2004 I have taught an undergraduate course at Notre Dame with the same title as this book. The idea of transforming that course into a book came from James Langford, for whose exceptional gifts as a publisher I have had reason to be grateful for many years. I thank him for his insights and advice. Not everything in this book has formed part of that course and not everything in that course forms part of this book. But I owe a large debt to five generations of students, over two hundred in number, who, by their questioning participation, helped to educate me, especially by compelling me to confront *their* questions posed in *their* terms. Whatever this book's defects, they have made it significantly better than it would otherwise have been and I am most grateful. Others who have helped to improve it significantly by their critical and constructive comments are my colleagues, Fred Freddoso, Brad Gregory, Ralph McInerny, David Solomon, and especially John O'Callaghan. I thank them for their generosity.

I am also extraordinarily grateful to Claire Shely for her secretarial work in helping to produce this book; to Tracy Westlake, administrative assistant in the Center for Ethics and Culture at Notre Dame; to Randy Yoho, who kept my computer from early retirement; to David Davidson, without whom Flanner Hall would not function; and to all those who clean offices, deliver mail, cook food, and so keep in being the university in which I have had the opportunity to write.

Alasdair MacIntyre
Mishawaka, Indiana
August 2008

GOD, PHILOSOPHY, UNIVERSITIES

CHAPTER ONE

~

God

How am I going to use the word 'God?' I will use it as its Hebrew, Greek, or Arabic equivalents were used by Abraham, by Isaiah, and by Job, by John and Paul, and by Muhammad. I am, therefore, not going to use it in the plural, as words translatable by 'god' were used by Aeschylus and by Horace, by the author of the *Ramayana* and by the Mayans. God, as understood by theists, by Jews, Christians, and Muslims, is necessarily One,the one and only God. Were he not such, he would not be God, for, if he exists, there can be no other who can set limits to the exercise of his powers or who can compare with him as an object worthy of our loving devotion. And so the psalmist could speak of God as a great king above all gods.

I say "if He exists," but, if he exists, he exists necessarily—that is to say, he could not have not existed. And in this he is unlike finite beings who exist and are what they are contingently, that is, they might have been otherwise than they are and they might not have existed at all. Moreover finite beings are limited in their powers and in their perfections. God, so understood, is limited in neither.

He is therefore unlimited in his power to act and there is nothing that can be known that he does not know. Nothing happens without his sustaining will and nothing can be thought or said or done of which he is unaware. He is perfect not only in his power and knowledge, but also in his goodness. Of his perfections we can form only imperfect conceptions, but the goodness ascribed to him is such that he is understood to will the good of all finite beings. And finite beings who possess the power of understanding, if they know that God exists, know that he is the most adequate object of their love, and that the deepest desire of every such being, whether they acknowledge it or not, is to be at one with God.

To believe that God, so understood, exists, is very different from believing in several gods, each of whom has limited powers, or from believing in one god whose powers are limited, or from believing in two gods, one of them presiding over a kingdom of light and the other over a kingdom of darkness, or from believing that the universe itself is divine. One difference is that none of these latter forms of belief generate three philosophical problems that are ineliminable from any version of theism.

The first of these is the problem of whether and how belief in the existence of God is compatible with recognition of the extent of natural, social, and moral evil in the universe of finite beings. It seems that the conjunction of the premises, "God is omnipotent" and "God wills the good of every finite being," entails the conclusion, "No evil occurs." But evil does occur. And it seems that the conjunction of the premises, "God is omnipotent" and "evil occurs," entails the conclusion, "God is responsible for evil." But in that case God is not—to say the least—unqualifiedly good. Theists are thereby confronted with the possibility that belief in God embodies a contradiction.

A second problem is that of whether and how belief in the existence of God is compatible with belief in the powers of finite beings, the powers that belong to inanimate objects, the powers that belong to animal bodies, and the powers of rational will that belong to human beings. For, if God is omnipotent and everything that happens, happens by his will, then God is the cause of every happening. But, if this is so, then it seems that finite beings do not in fact have any real powers. It is not that magnets attract iron filings, but that God moves the iron filings toward magnets. It is not that moles tunnel, but that God moves their limbs and that God opens up tunnels. Every event has God as its immediate cause, including those events that are human actions. God makes it the case that I decide to raise my hand and then God makes it the case that my hand rises. The finite universe is a puppet show and God is the puppet master.

Yet this conclusion is in fact at odds with any version of theism according to which God can justly hold human beings accountable for their actions. For, if human beings are to be so accountable, they must be able to exercise their powers as rational beings, to understand a good deal about the order of things, to act on the basis of their understanding, and by so doing to be agents of change. What happens in the world must be, in part, up to human beings. Such theists also characteristically believe that other types of finite being, including magnets and moles, have real powers of their own. So those of us who are theists of this kind—the vast majority of theists—are bound to reject any view of the universe as a divinely contrived puppet show. Consequently, we have the problem of reconciling our account of the independent powers of finite beings with our belief in God's omnipotence.

A third problem is of a different kind. When we speak of God's power or knowledge or goodness as unbounded, we raise the question of what we can mean when we ascribe these attributes to God, for we first learned to use the words 'power,' 'knowledge,' and 'goodness,' of a variety of finite beings, so that the power, knowledge, or goodness that we ascribed was always limited. Someone is powerful in this respect but not in another, knows this but not that, is good in some ways but not in others. And even when we use comparatives and superlatives and rank order the more and less powerful, knowledgeable, and good we still conceive of the power of the most powerful, the knowledge of the best informed, and the goodness of the very best of finite beings as having limits. What then can we mean when we speak of "unlimited" power or knowledge or goodness? Theists in recognizing that God exceeds the grasp of our understanding must also recognize that in trying to speak of God we are extending our use of words and the application of our concepts, so that we no longer understand what we mean when we talk about God to the same extent and in the same way that we do in our speech about finite beings. Is it then the case that in attempting to speak about God we have carried our analogizing beyond the limits of linguistic possibility and deprived our language of meaning? Here is a third inescapable problem for theists.

It is important to note that all three problems—those of evil, of the independence of finite beings, and of how to speak meaningfully about God—are internal to theism, not just problems posed from some external standpoint by critics dismissive of theism. Those problems would still arise for theists, even if no one had ever been an atheist, thereby showing that theism is philosophically problematic. Yet at the same time it is evident that for many theists, whether they are aware of the difficulties and complexities involved in these problems or not, their theistic belief is nonetheless unproblematic. Those who take themselves to have encountered God agree in finding it impossible to entertain serious doubts about his existence in very much the way that we are all of us unable to entertain serious doubts about the existence of our family and friends, even during periods in which we find those philosophical riddles known as the Other Minds problem (such as "How do we know that what seem to us to be other human beings are not in fact mechanical automata, constructed so that they simulate perfectly the appearance of beings with thoughts and feelings?") insoluble.

Yet those who are unaware of any experience in which they might have encountered God generally believe that this is so, not because of any failure of awareness on their part, let alone because of any decision by God to leave them severely alone, but because there is no God to be encountered. God, so they believe, is a figment of superstitious imaginations. And, since such atheists are often quite as intelligent and perceptive as, and sometimes more intelligent and perceptive than, most theistic believers, the question must arise, for theists just as much as atheists, as to whether theism is not after all a set of illusions. I set that question on one side, however, in order to take note of another central feature of theistic belief. Theistic belief is not just belief that there happens to exist a being with such and such attributes, a belief such that someone might allow that there is indeed such a being, but then say, "So what? God exists, as do neutrons and coconuts, but I happen to be interested in none of them." Of such a one theists would have to say that he is not using the word "God" as they use it, for to believe that God exists is to believe that there is a being on my relationship to whom depends everything that I do or might value. And this being requires of me unqualified trust and unqualified obedience, so that I cannot be indifferent to claims about His existence and nature. We finite beings would not exist if God had not created us. We would not continue to exist if he did not sustain us. The outcome of our every project and the fulfillment of our every desire depend on him. Or so theists believe.

Their belief, thus, has a double aspect, at once problematic and unproblematic. As the former, it invites ruthless and systematic questioning. As the latter, it requires devoted and unquestioning obedience. Theists who recognize one of these aspects of theism, but not the other, have an imperfect understanding of their own beliefs. Yet it seems impossible to acknowledge both aspects without tension and conflict. So theists have, it seems, a dilemma. Either they must willfully ignore some aspect of their own beliefs or they must live as divided selves, agonizing over the incompatible attitudes to which their beliefs give rise. Is there any way out of this dilemma?

CHAPTER TWO

~

Philosophy

Plain persons in our society think of philosophers as very different from themselves—and about the professional teachers of philosophy in contemporary universities they are manifestly right. Yet the obvious differences between the two in idiom, in mode of argument, in projects and preoccupations should not be allowed to obscure the relationship between questions asked by philosophers and some of the questions asked by plain persons. All human beings, whatever their culture, find themselves confronted by questions about the nature and significance of their lives: What is our place in the order of things? Of what powers in the natural and social world do we need to take account? How should we respond to the facts of suffering and death? What is our relationship to the dead? What is it to live a human life well? What is it to live it badly?

Yet characteristically these existential questions are raised for most human beings in the early history of humankind not as questions to be asked, let alone puzzled over, but as questions that have already received definitive religious answers. Those answers have of course varied from culture to culture. And they are generally presented through rituals, myths, and poetic narratives, which constitute the collective response of a culture to those questions. Philosophy is in the offing for the first time when someone asks whether something hitherto commonly and unquestioningly taken to be a religious truth is in fact true. How that comes to be asked also varies. Sometimes it is when, perhaps through contact with some alien culture, people become aware of some set of beliefs that provide alternative and rival answers to those existential questions. And sometimes it is because something happens that elicits a recognition of incoherence in a set of beliefs that had up till now been taken for granted. But on either type of occasion it is not just that the question of truth is raised—and once it is raised it rarely goes away—but that it becomes clear, as it was not earlier, that our differing beliefs about the nature and order of our lives and of the universe are rival answers to one and the same set of existential questions. And so it becomes possible to articulate those questions and to recognize that there are rival answers to them.

Attempts to find an answer to the question "But is it true?" inevitably lead on to two other questions: "Do we have sufficient reason to assert it?" and "What do we mean when we assert it?" For it seems that only if we can answer the third question will we be able to answer the second. And only if we can answer the second will we be able to answer the first. So truth, rational justification, and meaning become, from the outset, preoccupations of philosophers. And because they therefore need to understand what truth, rational justification, and meaning are, philosophy acquires its own distinctive problems. In order to deal with these, philosophers have to devise new and distinctively philosophical idioms and modes of argument and enquiry. So from the beginning philosophy has two aspects.

Its problems are, on the one hand, an extension of thoughts that may be elicited from any reflective individual, when the beliefs that she or he has so far taken for granted are put in question. Those who have hitherto unreflectively rank ordered the goods that they hope to achieve may now find themselves asking, "Are those the goods that it is best for me to pursue? Is this the right way to live?" And those who have hitherto accepted their assigned place in the social order may now ask: "Is this order just?" When such enquiries are pursued systematically, they become philosophical enquiries, while also remaining the enquiries of the plain persons who initially opened them up. Viewed in this light, philosophy answers questions that are or should be of interest to everyone. Yet philosophy has another aspect: that of a semitechnical, specialized form of activity into which one has to be initiated, so that one becomes able to speak in its peculiar idioms and to argue in its distinctive modes. And those who are successfully initiated thereby separate themselves not only from other plain persons, but also from the plain persons that they themselves once were and that in other areas of life they continue to be.

One danger confronting philosophers is that they may forget that their enquiries begin from and extend the enquiries of plain persons and that they are exercising their philosophical skills on behalf of those same plain persons. Philosophers have their own craft, but, like the practitioners of other crafts, such as fishing crews and construction workers, they can practice it for the common good—or they can fail to do so. If they do practice it for the common good, then they will take the trouble to engage in sustained conversation with plain persons, so as not to lose sight of the relationship between their enquiries, no matter how sophisticated, and the questions initially posed by plain persons. Yet, insofar as they include those who are not professional philosophers in their enquiries, they will make those plain persons painfully aware, if they were not already, that there are rival and incompatible answers to their questions and that philosophical enquiry is therefore a source of conflict.

Philosophers disagree with each other and have so disagreed from the beginning. And no matter how well developed their arguments in favor of some particular conclusion may be, there is never a point at which such a conclusion becomes invulnerable to further argument from some alternative and rival point of view. So that in philosophy the most that we are all of us entitled to claim for any conclusion or argument is that it is the best supported conclusion so far or the best argument so far. There are of course some conclusions that we are all of us entitled to hold with justifiable certainty. But even with these we have to be aware of and prepared to listen to arguments in favor of alternative and rival conclusions. We have to remain open to possible correction even by those with whom we are in fundamental disagreement.

CHAPTER THREE

~

God and philosophy

Belief in God has a much longer history than does the practice of philosophy. Even when philosophical enquiry emerges in different parts of the world, it is hundreds of years before one form of it, the Greco-Roman, post-Socratic form, encounters the beliefs and practices of theists. Yet we do not have to know very much about the long history generated by that encounter, or rather by a series of such encounters, to recognize that, at first sight at least, belief in God and an acceptance of the norms of philosophical enquiry seem to be incompatible. Why so?

The God of theism requires of those who acknowledge him unqualified trust and allegiance. When he discloses himself to us, it is as one who speaks only the truth, and what he discloses in word or deed it would be deeply foolish to deny or even to question. This is why the psalmist calls someone who says that there is no God a fool. But the thought that perhaps there is no God is one that philosophers are bound to take seriously. There are, *pace* Descartes, no knock-down arguments that will allow us to dismiss it once and for all. And even philosophers whose enquiries lead them to the conclusion that God does exist, and that he is who and what theistic believers say that he is, have to recognize that, insofar as their belief is supported by argument, it has no more philosophical warrant than that provided by the argument. Every assertion is to be treated as open to questioning, including those assertions that either describe or are part of God's self-disclosure. This is why belief in God appears to be incompatible with the norms governing philosophical enquiry.

There are three possible responses to this apparent incompatibility. A theistic believer who takes it to be not only apparent, but real, will respond by denying the claims of philosophy. And there have been such believers among Jews, Christians, and Moslems. Philosophers who agree with such believers in taking this incompatibility to be real may respond by denying the claims of theism, not in the name of some form of dogmatic unbelief, but as those who, even if they were prepared to entertain the truth of theism tentatively, would be precluded by their philosophical stance from holding *any* belief with the full and unqualified assent of theists. And there certainly have been such philosophers. The only remaining possibility is that the incompatibility is not in fact real. What grounds might there be for asserting this?

There are and have been theists according to whom it is the will and command of God that we should pursue philosophical enquiry into the nature of things and therefore into his existence and nature. On this view God created human beings as rational, that is, as questioning, animals. Among the goods that in virtue of our specific created nature we pursue is that of truth and we are required to pursue the truth concerning God's existence and nature through philosophical enquiry. I remarked earlier that theism has problems internal to it, such problems as that of evil, that of the independence of finite beings, and that of how to speak meaningfully about God, problems among those that theistic philosophers cannot but grapple with, pledged as they are to follow the argument wherever it may lead. In so doing they are bound, at some stages of their enquiry at least, to treat God's existence and nature as problematic. Yet they are to do so just because God has, so they believe, unproblematically presented himself to them as someone who commands them to do this. Is this complex set of attitudes possible? It is so only if faith in God, that is, trust in his word, can include faith that, even when one is putting God to the question, one can be praising him by doing so and can expect to be sustained by him in that faith. And it is so only if philosophical enquiry can enable us to move toward some significant resolution of the problems posed by theistic belief. But are such faith and such enquiry possible? The answer lies in the history of theistic philosophy, Jewish, Christian, and Islamic. But, before we turn to considering some aspects of that history, it is necessary to say more about the scope of theistic philosophical enquiry.

~

CHAPTER FOUR

God, philosophy, universities

Universities of course have a much shorter history than either theism or philosophy: in Islam from the ninth century onward, in Byzantium from the eleventh century, in Western Europe from the twelfth and thirteenth centuries. From the outset their forms of organization, their curricula, and their modes of teaching presuppose answers to questions that are central to the projects of theistic philosophical enquiry, questions about the relationships of philosophy both to theology and to the whole range of secular academic disciplines.

Theism, as I noted at the outset, is not just a set of doctrines about God. It concerns the nature of the natural and social universe as created and sustained by God, as embodying his purposes. For theists understanding how things are is inseparable from understanding them as informed by God's purposes. So any study of physics or history or political science or psychology that omits all reference to God will be importantly incomplete. And this puts theists at odds with any purely secular understanding of such academic disciplines. Yet what would it be instead to understand them in the terms afforded by a theistic account of the order and nature of things?

Any organized and institutionalized scheme of learning presupposes some view of how the various academic disciplines do or do not relate to each other. And so it is with universities. Consider in this light two very different types of university. In contemporary American universities each academic discipline is treated as autonomous and self-defining, so that its practitioners, or at least the most prestigious and influential among them, prescribe to those entering the discipline what its scope and limits are. And, in order to excel in any one particular discipline, one need in general know little or nothing about any of the others. Indeed, since prestige and influence most often attach to intensely and narrowly specialized research and scholarship, it would be imprudent for those who hope to excel in, say history, to expend the time and trouble needed to learn about physics—except of course for those who are historians of contemporary physics.

What is true of history and physics in contemporary American universities is also true of theology and philosophy. They too have become almost exclusively specialized and professionalized disciplines. To whom then in such a university falls the task of integrating the various disciplines, of considering the bearing of each on the others, and of asking how each contributes to the overall understanding of the nature and order of things? The answer is "No one," but even this answer is misleading. For there is no sense in the contemporary American university that there is such a task, that something that matters is being left undone. And so the very notion of the nature and order of things, of a single universe, different aspects of which are objects of enquiry for the various disciplines, but in such a way that each aspect needs to be related to every other, this notion no longer informs the enterprise of the contemporary American university. It has become an irrelevant concept. It makes little difference in this respect whether a university is professedly secular or professedly Catholic. Consider by contrast the Marxist universities of the Soviet Union or of Communist Eastern Europe between 1917 and 1991 and put aside for a moment the issues raised by their corruption by the pseudo-Marxism of Stalinist and post-Stalinist state power. They were of course atheistic and anti-theistic universities, but their atheism was not something merely negative, a denial of God's existence. It was a consequence of the dialectical and historical materialist understanding of the nature of things that provided them with a framework within which each of the academic disciplines could find its due place. So physics, history, and economics were all taught in a way that made their mutual relevance clear, and Marxist philosophy was assigned the tasks both of spelling out this relevance in contemporary terms and of explaining how the philosophies of the past had failed, just because they were the ideologically distorted expressions of class societies.

Theists of course are deeply critical of those aspects of Marxism that issue in Marxist atheism. And theists of different standpoints have leveled a variety of particular criticisms against particular Marxist theses. Nonetheless they have had to recognize that Marxism is a theory or a set of theories with the same scope as their own and that in responding to it they are responding to a theoretical atheism that is in some ways intellectually more congenial than the practical atheism of contemporary American universities. For by either eliminating mention of God from the curriculum altogether (departments of religious studies concern themselves with various types of belief in God, not with God), or by restricting reference to God to departments of theology, such universities render their secular curriculum Godless. And this Godlessness is, as I already noted, not just a matter of the subtraction of God from the range of objects studied, but also and quite as much the absence of any integrated and overall view of things.

What would it be for a university not to be Godless in this way? Its curriculum would have to presuppose an underlying unity to the universe and therefore an underlying unity to the enquiries of each discipline into the various aspects of the natural and the social. Over and above the questions posed in each of these distinct disciplinary enquiries—the questions of the physicist or the biologist or the historian or the economist—there would be questions about what bearing each of them has on the others and how each contributes to an overall understanding of the nature of things. Theology would be taught both for its own sake and as a key to that overall understanding. And it would be a central task of philosophy in such a university to enquire into the nature of the relationship between theology and the secular disciplines.

Philosophy is in any case a social and not a solitary form of enquiry. It requires a setting in which different and rival answers to philosophical questions can be proposed and objections to each considered in detail, so that such answers may be revised or rejected and such objections themselves subjected to critical scrutiny. And, if the enquiries of philosophy are to be sustained enquiries, as they need to be, they must be continued through different philosophical generations, each of which in turn has to be introduced through teaching to the enquiries and debates that have made philosophical questions what they have become in that particular time and place. Moreover philosophy cannot but draw upon the findings and insights of other disciplines. So that the type of institutionalized setting in which it is most likely to flourish is that of a college or university. Yet it makes a very great difference to how the relationship of philosophy to those other disciplines is understood whether the colleges and universities that provide the setting for its enquiries do or do not presuppose some kind of unity to the order of things, and, if so, what kind of unity.

Scott Soames has said of contemporary analytic philosophy that it "has become an aggregate of related, but semi-independent investigations, very much like other academic disciplines" and that "gone are the days of large, central figures, whose work is accessible and relevant to, as well as read by, all analytic philosophers. Philosophy has become a highly organized discipline, done by specialists primarily for other specialists" (Soames 2003, 2:463). Such highly professionalized specialized activities in which philosophers almost exclusively work within some particular subdiscipline or sub-subdiscipline are, as Soames notes, very much at one with the curriculum and the forms of organization of the contemporary university. The fragmentation of enquiry and the fragmentation of understanding are taken for granted. So that, if philosophy is to put them in question, as any theistic philosophy must, it must not only engage in distinctively different types of enquiry, but provide those enquiries, so far as it can, with a different type of academic setting.

Reference

Soames, Scott. *Philosophical Analysis in the Twentieth Century*. Princeton, NJ: Princeton University Press, 2003, 2:463.

PROLOGUES TO
THE CATHOLIC
PHILOSOPHICAL TRADITION

CHAPTER FIVE

~

Augustine

What then is it to be not just a theistic, but a Catholic philosopher? The first systematic answer to this question was given by St. Augustine, himself primarily a theologian, but also a practitioner of philosophy both in the ancient and in the modern senses of that word. In the Roman Empire *philosophia* was the name of a way of life. Those who participated in that way of life did so in the company of others who shared their views as to the ends of human life, the nature of the virtues, the kind of knowledge of those ends and those virtues that we are able to achieve. So to be a Platonist or an Aristotelian, a Stoic or an Epicurean was not only to adopt a theoretical standpoint. It was also to belong to a community of enquirers who aspired to live out the doctrines to which they gave their allegiance.

When Christianity appears on the scene, it is sometimes understood as one more example of a philosophy, one more community with its own authoritative teacher about the ends of life and the nature of things, a school of philosophy that is at odds with every other school of philosophy. And so from an early stage, Christian theologians find themselves in argumentative contention with the exponents of incompatible philosophies, but they also find that they are able to draw upon the argumentative resources of some of those schools in elucidation and defense of their own positions, and of those none more so than the Platonists. Yet at the same time they are in radical disagreement with some central Platonic claims. So in book 7 of the *Confessions*, Augustine contrasts what he was able to learn from "the books of the Platonists" and what he could learn only from the Christian revelation.

Some Christian truths he understands as prefigured in the Platonic texts. Others were such that no Platonists could have countenanced them. The Platonists can speak to us, as St. John does in the opening sentences of his gospel, of the invisible Word, but they cannot speak to us, as St. John does, of the Word made flesh.

In recognizing affinities between Platonism and Christianity, Augustine had of course had notable and authoritative predecessors. When fourth-century Catholic theologians engaged in debates with the followers of Arius, who held that the Son was created by the Father, debates that issued in the formulation of the Catholic doctrines of the Trinity and the Incarnation, they found themselves compelled to draw on the conceptual resources of Greek and especially Platonic philosophy. So it was with Athanasius's explanation and defense of the doctrine of the Trinity, as defined by the Council of Nicaea in 325. And so it was too in the writings of Basil, Gregory of Nyssa, and Gregory Nazianzen, the three Cappadocian theologians. In the debates about the Incarnation, whose definition took on final form at the Council of Chalcedon in 451, the same philosophical resources were needed: concepts of essence, nature, substance, and unity, largely drawn from Platonic sources. When, many centuries later, those seventeenth- and eighteenth-century heirs of the fourth-century Arians, the English Unitarians, looked for the source of Trinitarian error, they found it in what they took to be the corruption of primitive Christianity by Platonism (see Priestley 1782).

Yet of course Platonism was, in key respects, as Augustine had recognized, at odds with Catholic Christianity. The writings of the Platonists provided arguments for the rejection of materialism, and the young Augustine had been a materialist. "I was so gross of mind," he said of his earlier self, "not seeing even myself clearly—that whatever was not extended in space, either diffused or massed together or swollen out or having some such qualities or at least capable of having them, I thought must be nothing whatsoever" (Sheed 1993, 7.1.107). But, while he seems to have been convinced by Platonist arguments, especially Plotinus's, that there are immaterial beings, indeed that we as minds and souls are such beings, what, if he is to become a Christian, he has to reject is the Platonist belief that souls are harmed and diminished by their contacts with bodies. For Plotinus the Divine Word could not have become flesh, while Augustine held that "God made the body good, for He is good" (Sheed ps. 141, 18).

The question therefore arises as to whether and how it is possible for Christians to accept from Platonism that which supports and illuminates Christian belief while rejecting what is incompatible with it. Consider in this respect the argument that Plotinus had advanced in the Seventh Tractate of the *Fourth Ennead*, which Augustine had read in Latin translation. (I am indebted to John Haldane's discussion of Plotinus's argument in his "(I am) thinking" in *Ratio* [16, 2, June 2003], although I understand it somewhat differently.)

Plotinus conceived of the human soul as having a range of powers, powers of sense perception, which put it in touch with the lower world of bodies, powers of discursive reasoning, which it is able to put to a variety of uses, and powers of intellectual apprehension, in the exercise of which it becomes one with *Nous*, eternal mind (*Enneads* 4, passim; my interpretation of Plotinus in general follows Hilary Armstrong 1999). Plotinus argues to the conclusion that the human soul cannot be, or be produced by, any body or collocation of bodies (*Enneads* 4.7.2). He identifies as the relevant characteristic of the human soul, one essential to its unity, its self-awareness (*Enneads* 4.7.3).

It is not just, on Plotinus's view, that the human soul is capable of becoming aware of its own activities of thinking and feeling, but that in its progress toward the divine different modes of self-awareness play a key part. So someone who is as yet "unable to see himself," but who becomes aware of what is divine within him, sees an image of himself as "lifted to a better beauty." Yet, if he is to become one with the divine in power and will, he has to put that image aside. Insofar as he sees the divine as external to himself, "There can be no vision unless in the sense of identification with the object. And this identification amounts to a self-knowing, a self-awareness. . . ." More generally, "We are most completely aware of ourselves when we are most completely identified with the object of our knowledge" (translations from MacKenna 1958, 5.8.11).

Plotinus connects the self-awareness of the human soul with its unity, arguing that the unity of the soul is quite other than the unity of a body, since the relationships of bodies to each other and of parts of bodies to each other lack the characteristics that give the human soul its unity. In what does the unity of a human soul consist? It involves at least this: that in many of its acts and experiences I am or can be aware of myself as acting and experiencing, so that I cannot but refer to myself as one and the same as the author of those acts and the undergoer of those experiences. To put this in terms that are other than Plotinus's: it is not just that the 'I' of "I think that" and "I judge that" and "I feel that" is one and the same 'I,' with one and the same reference, but that all these are one and the same 'I' with one and the same reference as the 'I' of "I am aware that I think," "I am aware that I judge," and so on. And the human soul is partially constituted as the kind of being that it is by this identity of reference.

Nothing in the composition of a material being, a body, or in the unity of a body, corresponds to this. We nowadays do not of course hold the same beliefs as Plotinus did about the material world. He could write that "very certainly matter does not mould itself to pattern or bring itself to life" (7.4.3). But we have the best of reasons to believe that under certain types of conditions matter does just these things. Stuart A. Kaufmann has summarized one version of this belief by saying that "life is an expected, emergent property of complex chemical reaction networks" (2000, 35). What emerge are autonomous agents and "An autonomous agent, or a collection of them in an environment is a nonequilibrium system that propagates some new union of matter, energy, constraint construction, measurement, record, information, and work" (107). In some of these autonomous agents "mere chemistry . . . can harbor symbols and signs in the full sense of the words" (112). Indeed, were it not so, we could not speak of the transmission of, for example, genetic information as we do. So Plotinus's beliefs about matter were false. But none of this undermines Plotinus's argument about the human soul.

All the examples of the transmission of genetic or other information by molecules, plants, bacteria, and insects cited by Kaufmann are not only examples of entities whose symbolizing and signaling activities involve no kind of self-awareness, but of entities whose material condition can be identified prior to and independently of their symbolizing and signaling powers, while the human soul, as characterized by Plotinus, is not only self-aware, but has no being apart from those activities of thought of which it always can be and often is aware. Hence the unity of the soul is quite other than the unity of any body, whether that physicochemical unity is understood as Plotinus understood it or as we nowadays understand it.

Plotinus also held that the matter without which bodies would not exist as bodies is evil, and that it is through involvement with the material world that souls become evil. Yet nothing in Plotinus's argument about the soul implies, let alone entails, that matter is evil or a source of evil and there is no inconsistency in both affirming the goodness of the material universe and accepting Plotinus's conclusions about the soul. (Indeed there would be nothing inconsistent in accepting those conclusions and also affirming that the human soul is by its nature essentially embodied.)

What was required of Augustine was that he, as a Christian, should be able to provide an alternative account of the nature of evil in the soul. And this he did by locating human evil in the will. The effect of original sin is that the will of each and every individual is informed by sin, notably by the sin of pride. So misdirected the will aims at other than its goods, generating destructive and self-destructive conflict, unable to attain the peace that all human beings desire. No one can rescue themselves from this condition, for to do so would require an act of will. But every act of will is infected by the very condition from which the will needs to be rescued. Only by God's grace can the will be transformed, so that it is no longer informed by pride, but by charity.

What God's grace summons and enables those who receive it to achieve is a redirection of the whole human being, so that the exercise of our bodily powers, as well as of our powers of mind and spirit, give expression to the will's transformation, a transformation that always remains incomplete in this present life. Even though our bodies are, as a result of God's punishment for sin, subject to death and to a variety of ills, it is as embodied beings that we are directed toward God. Augustine's theology is therefore at odds both with the materialism that the Platonists had taught him to reject and with the Platonic dualism of soul and body, with its denigration of the body. And Augustine had recognized that the refutation of these twin and opposing errors is a task for philosophy.

Philosophical enquiry by itself cannot provide us with an adequate knowledge either of God or of ourselves. What it can do is to give us sufficient reason to reject those philosophical conclusions that are at variance with the Catholic faith. Philosophical arguments had played a key part in Augustine's criticism of his own earlier Manichean beliefs. And it had provided him with grounds for rejecting the skepticism of the New Academy, grounds that he set out in the first book that he wrote after his conversion, *Contra Academicos*, in order to explain why he now was able to hold as certain the doctrines of the Catholic faith.

The philosophers of the New Academy, most notably Arcesilaus and Carneades, had argued that nothing can be certainly known and that the wise will neither assent to nor deny any proposition. So famously, during a visit to Rome in 156/5 B.C., Carneades had argued on one day that justice is a natural virtue and on the next that it is no more than a matter of convention, dictated by expediency. We can indeed, the Academic skeptics allowed, judge certain propositions to be more plausible than others and these provide us with a basis for action. But certainty we cannot achieve. Augustine had become aware of these sceptical claims through reading Cicero's *Academica* and in the first book of the *Contra Academicos* he posed the question of whether it is possible to attain happiness while still only a searcher for truth rather than as one who has achieved it. It is because of their relevance to this question that Augustine examines the central theses of the Academic sceptics and his aim is to show that there are some truths that can be known with unqualified certainty. His most interesting argument runs as follows.

The sceptics had relied on Zeno's contention that only that which has no mark in common with what is false can be true (Garvey 3.9.18, pp. 62–63). And they had then argued that everything claimed to be true has some mark in common with what is false, so that nothing can be certainly known. Augustine argues that either Zeno's thesis is true or it is false. If it is true, then there is something that can be certainly known, namely Zeno's thesis. If it is false, then it gives us no reason to assert that nothing can be certainly known. But what can be certainly known is that either it is true or it is false and therefore something can be certainly known. Augustine then proceeds to make objections designed to undermine skeptical doubt about the testimony of sense experience, arguing that we are deceived by the senses only if we do not limit our assent to what we take to be true on the basis of sense experience. So I am deceived by the visual appearance of the oar in the water that seems to be bent, but is in fact straight, only if I judge incautiously.

Sense experience is the starting point for our knowledge. And, when the mind moves beyond sense experience, it moves from within itself, from an awareness of what it is of which the mind is aware in sense experience, toward a knowledge of forms, conceived very much as Plato conceived them, except that for Augustine they are ideas in the mind of God. To grasp the forms and so to render what is presented to the mind intelligible, the mind has to receive light from God. Without this divine illumination we cannot achieve even natural knowledge. So God is present to the mind, even when still unperceived by it.

Augustine returned to the problems of skepticism later in life. In book 11 of *De Civitate Dei*, written in 417 when he was sixty-three years old, he argued that it is because we are made in the image of God that "we both are, and know that we are, and delight in our being, and our knowledge of it" (11.26). Augustine immediately adds, "In respect of these truths, I am not at all afraid of the arguments of the Academics, who say, What if you are deceived? For if I am deceived, I am. For he who is not, cannot be deceived. . . ." So Descartes's later "Cogito, ergo sum" is anticipated by Augustine's "Si fallor, sum." But Augustine goes on very differently from Descartes, arguing that I am deceived neither in believing that I know nor in believing that I love. What I love may not be what I take it to be, but that I love it, whatever it is, is certain.

Yet here again philosophical argument has primarily a negative function, that of providing us with grounds for rejecting conclusions that would otherwise bar the way to further enquiry. What it cannot do by itself is to initiate that enquiry or carry it further. How then are we to proceed? "If someone says to me, I would understand in order that I may believe, I answer, Believe, that you may understand" (Sermons, Among Which a Series on Selected Lessons of the New Testament 43.3.4). This is a recurrent thought in Augustine. What he meant by it he explained in *De ordine*, written soon after *Contra Academicos*: "We are guided in a twofold way, by authority and by reason. In time authority comes first; in matter, reason. So it follows that authority opens the door to those who desire to learn the great and hidden good. And whoever enters by it . . . will at length learn how preeminently possessed of reason are those things which were the object of his pursuit before he saw their reason, and what that reason itself is which now that he has become firm and capable in the cradle of authority, he now follows and understands" (2.9.26).

There is no chain of philosophical reasoning or method of philosophical enquiry through which we can arrive at the truths of faith as conclusions. But once by faith we have acknowledged those truths we are able to understand why there is good reason to acknowledge them. This, as he was to argue a little later, is because of the effects of sin on the human mind. It is "because human minds are obscured by familiarity with darkness, which covers them in a night of sins and bad habits, and are unable to perceive with the clarity and purity proper to reason" that authority has been provided to bring "the faltering eye into the light of truth" (*De moribus ecclesiae catholicae* 31.2.31).

What Augustine means by this is best understood by considering his account of self-knowledge. In the *Soliloquies*, another of the works written soon after his conversion, he asks himself, "What then do you wish to know?" and he answers, "I desire to know God and the soul. Nothing more? Nothing at all" (1.7). And it turns out that these two kinds of knowledge are inseparable. Knowledge of one's soul is possible only in the light afforded by the knowledge of God. And knowledge of God that goes beyond that knowledge of God as creator of earth, sky, and sea which is possessed by every people (*Tractate XXIV on John's Gospel* 106.4) requires knowledge of God as present within the soul and so knowledge of the soul.

It is the whole soul, the whole mind, that knows. And in aspiring to know itself it aspires to know itself as a whole, to become aware of itself not just in this or that part or function, that is, as thought or meaning or desire or will, but as that which perceives, thinks, judges, remembers, feels, desires, and wills. The injunction "Know thyself" has this point and purpose, that only by knowing its own true nature can the mind live in accordance with that nature. Otherwise it will be at odds with itself. "For perverse desire makes it act often as though it had forgotten itself" (Burnaby 1955, 80).

To achieve self-understanding and self-knowledge—and also, it will turn out, knowledge of God—we therefore have to turn within. "Do not go abroad. Return within yourself. In the inward human being dwells truth. If you find that you are by nature mutable, transcend yourself" (*Of True Religion* 72). But we are only able to move within ourselves, so that we become aware of our true nature and transcend ourselves, if we receive from God by grace the means to do so. Otherwise the path to self-knowledge is closed to us. Why so? What deprives us of the knowledge of God also deprives us of self-knowledge: an indefinite capacity for distraction by external trivialities and a craving for self-justification, so that we either do not attend to what is within or, if we do, disguise from ourselves our thoughts and motives. And in areas where our sexuality exerts its power, we lose our capacity for self-examination (*Confessions* 10.35–37). It is God alone who can rid us of the pride and the desire that is at work in these various agencies of self-deception.

It is therefore important not just that the *Confessions* is written as a prayer, a prayer of narrative acknowledgment, but that it could only have been written as a prayer. It is only as Augustine puts himself into the hands of God that he can write truly and truthfully about himself, ridding himself of those distortions that are the expression of pride, for the will of fallen human beings is informed by pride until and unless divine grace rescues it from pride by informing it instead with charity. Belief is a precondition of grace, grace of charity, and charity of an undistorted vision of oneself and so of understanding.

Progress toward self-knowledge is progress in understanding the true objects of our desires. As I already noticed, Augustine thinks that I cannot be in error about the fact that I love, but that I may always be in error about what it is that I love. Augustine, like every other ancient author, whether pagan or Christian, takes the intensity of human desire for granted. It is because of that intensity that desire is so powerful an agent of unreason and self-deception. What we discover in our progress toward self-knowledge is that our desires are inordinate in respect of their finite objects, such objects as those of the bodily pleasures, of the goods of success and the goods of friendship. And they are inordinate because they are at once expressions of and disguises for our love of God. We repress in ourselves the knowledge that we are by nature directed toward God and the symptoms of that repression are the excessive and disproportionate regard that we have for objects that substitute themselves for God, objects which, when we achieve them, leave us disappointed and dissatisfied. It is only insofar as we make God the object of our desire, acknowledging that to desire otherwise is to desire against our nature, that our desires in general become rightly ordered and that we are rescued from the self-protection of a will informed by pride.

The present-day reader cannot but be reminded of Freud, whose account of sexuality and religion in some respects is an inversion of Augustine's. For Freud it is belief in God that is illusory. Our desires are indeed defective and failure to resolve infantile conflicts has resulted in an inability to recognize their true objects. As a result we have substituted false objects, among them God. In order to resolve the conflicts that issue in our neurotic symptoms, and sometimes in the psychoses, we have to undergo a discipline whose effect would be to leave us without belief in God. The contrast with Augustine is striking: for Freud belief in God is an illusion that disguises our distorted and inhibited sexual drives; for Augustine our distorted sexuality entangles us in illusions about the object of our desires, disguising our belief in and our desire for God. So how might we decide between these rival claims? Both Augustine and Freud have answers to this question and once again they are interestingly parallel, even if very different.

For both there is someone before whom and to whom one talks, so that in the end one's prevarications and concealments and self-justifications are heard as what they are and the truth about oneself, including the truth about one's resistance to acknowledging that truth, is acknowledged. In both cases the talking involves a discipline, in the one case that of prayer, in the other that of psychoanalysis. And both insist that there is no way of evaluating that particular discipline from a purely external point of view, for such evaluation will be frustrated by those same fantasies from which the discipline is designed to free us.

Of course not all psychoanalysts have followed Freud in viewing theistic belief as an illusion and there have been more than a few Catholic practitioners of psychoanalysis, something that might have shocked Freud himself. Moreover the parallels between the practice of prayer and the practice of analysis must not be pressed too far. Nonetheless they may help to illuminate Augustine's claims that prayer is the path to self-knowledge and the only adequate path to self-knowledge and self-understanding. Yet in order to achieve this understanding, we must first believe and believe in a way that commits us to the life of prayer.

Philosophy is thus at once independent of theology and yet dependent upon it in Augustine's scheme. It is independent insofar as it has its own standards of enquiry and argument. But it is dependent in that the point and purpose of its enquiries and the significance of the conclusions of its arguments can only be understood from within a theologically committed standpoint. And this double character of the relationship of philosophy to theology leaves it open to Augustine's successors to interpret his position in more than one way, so that there are both later Augustinians—notably

Aquinas—who treat philosophy as an independent form of enquiry, and later Augustinians who insist that philosophy has no legitimate place except within and subordinated to the theological enterprise.

Philosophy on Augustine's own view is a study preliminary to theology. When he lists the seven liberal arts in *Soliloquies*, they are grammar, rhetoric, logic, arithmetic, geometry, music, and astronomy, but in *Retractations* philosophy has replaced astronomy. By listing philosophy as a liberal art Augustine includes it among those studies whose skills must be acquired as a necessary preliminary to theological enquiry and as a helpful aid to the reading and interpretation of scripture. This is how he came to view his own education into the discipline of rhetoric. We can see his rhetorical as well as his philosophical skills at work in his final statement of the relationship of the philosophical enquiries of the pre-Christian ancient philosophers to Christianity in book 19 of the *De Civitate Dei*.

Augustine begins from the summary of ancient philosophy provided by M. T. Varro in his *De Philosophia*. Varro, who died in the year 27 B.C., was a writer of encyclopedic learning. Classifying the various and rival schools of philosophy according to their conceptions of the supreme good for human beings, Varro had calculated that there were 288 possible different conceptions of the supreme good, of how it was to be achieved, of whether it is an individual good, or one to be achieved and enjoyed only in the company of others, and of what kind of certainty respecting it could be attained. Augustine however finds reason to conclude that the vast majority of these 288 possibilities can be eliminated by philosophical argument and that we are then left with only three alternatives: that the life through which the supreme good is to be achieved is either a life in which virtue is pursued for its own sake, or it is a life of virtue pursued both for its own sake and for the sake of the goods of life, or it is a life in which the goods of life other than virtue are pursued for their own sake.

Reflection on these three alternatives leads Augustine to the further conclusion that the most adequate philosophical conception of the supreme good is that it consists of a life of virtue pursued both for its own sake and for the sake of the other goods of life, the goods both of body and of soul. Moreover it is a good that can be achieved and enjoyed only in the company of others. So far philosophical enquiry can take us, but no further. And a theological perspective brings to light the defects and the inadequacies of any purely philosophical, purely natural standpoint. For what we have learned from the Christian revelation is that blessedness is not to be had in this present life and that the exercise of the virtues does not achieve happiness. The virtues are engaged in an unending struggle with vices and evils and the most that we can expect from the possession of prudence, temperance, justice, and courage is that we will be able to avert certain evils, at least for the time being.

Moreover the social relationships into which we need to enter to achieve our good are themselves sources of anxiety and harm. We can never rely wholly on either our family and household or our friends. We are members of political communities in which justice is always mingled with injustice and in which perennially we find ourselves at war with other political communities. The true good is to be found only where peace is complete and unassailable and this is never so in this present life. Where it is so, we shall attain all the goods proper to our nature, goods of both body and spirit, and the virtues will thus be rewarded with victory in their struggle.

In this present life we are blessed insofar as we can attain that measure of peace that is possible for us. And true virtue, virtue informed by charity, is able to make good use of such peace and even of the evils that afflict us when such temporal peace is absent. Everyone desires peace. Even those who make war do so for the sake of achieving peace. And we very much want peace in our own households. But pride leads us to try to achieve this peace by imposing our will upon others and the peace thus achieved is the peace of the unjust, the peace of the earthly city of man, not the peace of the heavenly city of God.

Nonetheless even this peace bears witness to the truths that "there is no vice so clean contrary to nature that it obliterates even the faintest traces of nature" and that "even what is perverted must of necessity be in harmony with and in dependence on . . . the order of things" (19.12 De Civitate Dei). "There cannot be a nature in which there is no good" (19.13).

The law of nature preserves the peace that is the order of things through all distresses and disturbances. "The peace of all things is the tranquility of order" (19.13 De Civitate Dei), the order of the body, of animal life, of the appetites, of body and soul, of domestic peace, civil peace, and the peace of heaven. But our proneness to error is such that we can only enjoy these if we are obedient to God's eternal law and walk by faith, not by sight.

Augustine therefore concludes once again that philosophy by itself cannot afford us a true view of the order of things. But he continues to appeal to philosophical argument as well as to revealed truths, since philosophy understood from the standpoint of faith has an indispensable part to play in Christian thinking in spite of its limitations, limitations that philosophers cannot recognize except from the standpoint of faith. Yet philosophical enquiry, even unaided by faith, is a work of natural reason and nature is never wholly corrupted. So Augustine's final verdict on the philosophers of Greece and Rome was that, although they had made various mistakes, "nature itself has not permitted them to wander too far from the path of truth" in their judgments about the supreme good (*De Civitate Dei* 19.1).

Cited Works by Augustine

Contra Academicos (*Against the Skeptics*)
De Civitate Dei (*The City of God*)
De moribus ecclesiae catholicae et de moribus Manichaeorum (*On the Morals of the Catholic Church and on the Morals of the Manichaeans*)
De ordine (*On Order*)
De vera religione (*Of True Religion*)
In Iohannis evangelium tractatus (*Tractate XXIV on John's Gospel*)
Retractationes (*Retraction*)
Soliloquiorum Libri Duo (*Soliloquies*)

References

Armstrong, Hilary. "Aristotle in Plotinus: the Continuity and Discontinuity of *Psych* and *Nous*." *Oxford Studies in Ancient Philosophy*, supp. vol. Ed. J. Annas. Oxford: Clarendon Press, 1999.

Burnaby, J., trans. *Augustine: Later Works*. London: SCM Press, 1955.

Dod, M., trans. *The City of God*. New York: Random House, 1950.

Garvey, M. P., RSM, trans. *Against the Academicians*. Milwaukee, WI: Marquette University Press, 1957, III.

Kaufmann, Stuart A. *Investigations*. Oxford: Oxford University Press, 2000.

MacKenna, Stephen, trans. *The Enneads*. London: Faber & Faber, 1958.

Priestley, Joseph. *An History of the Corruptions of Christianity*. Birmingham: Piercy and Jones, 1782.

Sheed, F. J., trans. *Confessions*. Indianapolis, IN: Hackett, 1993.

CHAPTER 6

~

Boethius, the Pseudo-Dionysius, and Anselm

As a philosopher Augustine belongs to the history of ancient philosophy. Yet every history of medieval philosophy has to begin from his work, since his texts were throughout the Christian Middle Ages accorded an authority greater than any other outside sacred scripture. And when some eight hundred years later the rediscovery of Aristotle's metaphysics and ethics in the Latin West posed in the sharpest possible way the question of how philosophical enquiry was related to theological beliefs founded on an appeal to God's self-revelation, it was still Augustine's understanding of that relationship that set the terms for the ensuing debate. But that debate cannot be made fully intelligible without an awareness first of some philosophical episodes in the history of the Latin West between Augustine's age and the recovery of Aristotle and, second, of how, when Aristotle was rediscovered, it was to a significant extent Aristotle as understood by his Islamic commentators. So I shall consider each of these in turn, but first a warning is necessary.

It is not just that I will be writing a highly selective history, but that the selection will be aimed only at making the debates and enquiries of the thirteenth century intelligible and with them the genesis of the Catholic philosophical tradition. So I do not pretend to provide a history of either Latin or Islamic philosophy in the relevant period, not even a truncated and abbreviated history. Too many important thinkers will go unnoticed and much of the thought of those to whom I do attend will be ignored. With this warning I proceed to consider Boethius, the so-called Pseudo-Dionysius, and Anselm, in each case because of the resources that they provided for later Catholic thought. Anicius Manlius Severinus Boethius (ca. 480–524) set himself the task of making the works of both Aristotle and Plato available to the Latin and Roman educated public of his day. "Every work of Aristotle that has come into our hands . . . drawn from the art of logic, from the weighty consideration of moral experience, and from a shrewd and subtle understanding of the truth about nature," Boethius wrote in his commentary on Aristotle's *De Intepretatione*, "I shall translate into Latin and in the correct order. Moreover I shall throw light on all this by commentary and I shall also translate all Plato's dialogues and likewise comment on them, presenting them in Latin" (2.3). But Boethius's project was left radically incomplete.

He completed translations of Aristotle's *Categories*, the *Prior Analytics*, the *Posterior Analytics*, the *Sophistical Refutations*, and the *Topics*. And, in addition to his commentary on the *De Interpretatione*, he produced an elementary and an advanced commentary on the *Isagōgē*, an introduction to Aristotle's logic written by Plotinus's pupil, Porphyry. But Aristotle's other works and Plato's dialogues were left untranslated. Since Boethius died—executed by the Ostrogothic king of Italy, Theodoric, whose minister he had been—about the age of forty-five, this is unsurprising. What is surprising is how much else he achieved both philosophically and theologically, particularly when we consider how much of his time must have been spent in discharging the duties of public office, before he lost favor with the king.

He was deeply concerned with the form that an education in the liberal arts should take and wrote textbooks on geometry, arithmetic, and music. To him we owe the word *quadrivium*, the name adopted in the middle ages for the four disciplines that succeeded the *trivium* of grammar, rhetoric, and dialectic. Of the disciplines of the *quadrivium* Boethius asserted that without them it was impossible to achieve perfection in philosophical studies.

Boethius also wrote four, perhaps five, short theological works, defending Catholic doctrines. Indeed it may have been his Catholic allegiance that offended the Arian Theodoric. What is striking in his final and greatest work is his insistence on the autonomy of philosophy. *On the Consolation of Philosophy* was written while he was in prison awaiting execution. He portrays Philosophia as a woman, "My nurse in whose house I had been cared for since my youth," who comes to visit him in prison, driving away "those sluts," the Muses of poetry. He praises her arguments, because she unfolds them without any help "from without," that is, without employing anywhere as premises truths that cannot be vindicated by philosophical enquiry (3.12). Among such external truths are of course the revealed truths of the Catholic faith.

Boethius therefore, unlike Augustine, is committed to philosophy as an autonomous enterprise. He found neither opposition nor tension between the truths revealed to faith and the truths apprehended by reason. And so in *On the Consolation of Philosophy* what Philosophia discloses is an account of the universe as ordered by divine providence, of the God who orders it, and of the happiness that is to be found in God, an account that at no point appeals to Christian revelation. There have indeed been those who have argued that Boethius must therefore have ceased to be a Christian, in order to write as he did (see A. Momigliano 1955). But this is an implausible and unnecessary hypothesis (for an excellent discussion of the issues see Watts 1969).

It must already be clear how great the contrast is between Boethius and Augustine and this even though Boethius within theology aligned himself with Augustinian positions. This is as much a matter of the differences in their relations to the culture of which they were a part as it is of their real or apparent differences on philosophical and theological questions. Augustine is concerned to underline both the antagonism between pagan Rome and the city of God and the contrast between our present life on earth and our future life in heaven. In our present life we cannot escape from participation in the institutions of secular life, households, courts of justice, and the agencies of the Roman *imperium*. His emphasis is upon the flawed and radically imperfect character of these institutions, corrupted and distorted as they are by sin. Boethius would not perhaps have disagreed, but his perspective is different.

He speaks out of and to an educated society that understands itself as at once Christian and Roman. He came from a senatorial family and was proud to have been sole consul, when he was thirty, even prouder that his two sons were made joint consuls. For Theodoric had preserved in his kingdom—in fact independent, although nominally under the overlordship of the Byzantine emperor—many of the forms of Roman life and culture and even some of their substance. That substance it was Boethius's life work to preserve for future generations. Hence arose his concern both for the liberal arts and for the translation of Plato and Aristotle. The former represented the educational heritage of the ancient world, the latter its greatest thought. What then did he bequeath to his philosophical heirs?

First, he provided knowledge of Aristotle's logic and with it a sense, even if an inadequate sense, of what Aristotle had achieved, so that when, some centuries later, Aristotle's other works were recovered, it was a good deal easier than it would otherwise have been to come to terms with them. Second, one further result of this was a recognition once and for all of the importance of the study of logic for philosophical enquiry and its indispensable place in the earliest stages of a philosophical education. And, third, the image of philosophy presented in *Consolation* was so influential that the possibility of engaging in philosophy as an autonomous mode of enquiry, and not merely as part of the theological enterprise, was kept open in times and places to which it would otherwise have been an alien notion. That influence can scarcely be exaggerated. *On the Consolation of Philosophy* was not only read widely wherever Latin was read in the Western Middle Ages, it also was translated into Anglo-Saxon by King Alfred and, a good deal later, into French and German, Greek, Dutch, Provençal, Italian, and Spanish.

Yet Boethius's philosophical importance is not exhausted by these influences. What identifies him most importantly as a philosopher is the fact that he passed on to his successors—among them us—not only a set of conclusions, but a set of problems. In the *Isagōgē* Porphyry had posed a question about how species and genera are to be understood. Are they concepts that the human mind itself makes or do they exist prior to and independently of the mind? If they exist independently, are they material or immaterial and do they exist in or apart from the objects of our sense perceptions? Porphyry had set out alternative possibilities, but he had pressed the question no further. Boethius in his commentary on the *Isagōgē* goes one step beyond Porphyry.

He denies that, if species and genera are concepts made by the mind by an act of abstraction, they are therefore no more than fictions. We abstract geometrical concepts from sense experience, but they are not fictions as the notion of a centaur is the notion of a fiction: "Not every thought which is from a subject but not as that subject itself is must be false and empty" (Spade 1994, 23). The mind is capable of abstracting that which is incorporeal from the corporeal, as when we consider lines in purely geometrical terms, in abstraction from the bodies in which we perceive lines. "Consequently let no one say that, since the line cannot exist apart from bodies, we think of the line falsely when we grasp it mentally, as though it existed apart from bodies."

So it is too with species and genera. We perceive similarities in particulars, humanness in a variety of human beings. "This likeness, when considered by the mind and perceived in a true way, becomes a species" (Spade 1994, 23). And in like fashion we proceed from species to genera. Species and genera do not exist independently of and apart from particulars. They are brought into being by the mind's activity in perceiving and understanding those particulars and without them neither our perceptions nor our judgments could be what they are. In apprehending them we make the particulars that we perceive intelligible.

Boethius takes himself in setting out this position to be stating Aristotle's point of view. And he acknowledges that it is at odds with Plato's treatment of species and genera as existing prior to and independently of the mind's act of understanding. As to where the truth lies, with Plato or with Aristotle, Boethius makes no judgment. And in leaving open the issues that he takes to divide Plato from Aristotle, Boethius provides a crucial part of the later agenda for Catholic philosophy. The influence of Boethius's near contemporary, the late fifth-century philosopher whose texts were ascribed to St. Paul's first-century convert, Dionysius the Areopagite, and who is therefore commonly known as Pseudo-Dionysius, was of a very different kind. Dionysius was as much of a Neoplatonist as it is possible to be while also being a Christian. His Neoplatonism, which he learned from Proclus, provided him with much of his philosophical vocabulary. But he had also learned from the Cappadocian fathers and he wrote of the relationship of God to the world both in terms of emanation and in terms of creation. In four treatises and ten letters, he expounded three theologies, the Cataphatic which speaks of God as efficient cause, the Symbolic which speaks of God as final cause, and the Mystical which speaks of—or falls silent in relation to—God as he is in himself. The world of finite beings proceeds from God as first efficient cause and returns to God as ultimate final cause. And in speaking of God as cause we name him as good, as wise, as living, as he who is, as power, and as peace. What we cannot do is know God as he is in himself or name him as he is in himself, for only what we know can be named. How then are we to talk about God? Dionysius opens up the most fundamental of the philosophical problems about God.

The Mystical theology instructs us to proceed by taking each of the terms affirmed of God in the Cataphatic and Symbolic theologies and then denying that that term holds of God. Does this mean that we first made a mistake in affirming of God what we affirmed? The answer of Dionysius is surely: Not at all. It is only through first making these particular affirmations and then denying that they hold that we progress toward God. For our acts of naming God's attributes and then of denying that they hold of God are inseparable from a progress toward God in contemplative experience as well as in naming. Among the affirmations that we first make and then withhold is that God is. But in denying that this affirmation holds of God we are not denying God's existence as the atheist does. Of God, on the view taken by Dionysius, we cannot say either that he is or that he is not.

How then are we to construe Dionysius? What does he mean? Dionysius uses Platonic idioms. Like the Form of the Good in the *Republic*, and like the One of whom Plotinus speaks, God is said to exist beyond being. But how are we to understand this? The text gives us no answer. It is left to later commentators to provide a variety of interpretative answers and interpretations necessarily go beyond the text itself. But the text is one with which any adequate theology has to come to terms, if only because no theist can escape the force of Dionysius's claim that all the concepts through which we express our beliefs about God are inadequate, yet at the same time theistic belief cannot be expressed except through the use of such concepts. And existence is among the concepts with which a theist cannot dispense. Of God, if we believe in him, we cannot but say that he exists. Or perhaps we need to advance an even stronger contention. Since, if God exists, he exists necessarily, is it perhaps the case that the concept of God is such that, if we genuinely grasp it, we cannot but affirm that God exists? If this were the case, then it would be true of any atheist that either he has not grasped the concept of God, that, whatever he is denying, he is not denying that God exists, or else his denial of divine existence is conceptually incoherent. This strong thesis is entailed by the conclusion arrived at by the greatest of Augustine's later followers, Anselm (1033/4–1109).

Some of Anselm's philosophical arguments, and most notably his argument in the *Proslogion* for the existence of God, have been discussed by later philosophers as though they could be abstracted from the Augustinian theological context within which he advanced them. And in one way this is legitimate. Abstract the arguments from their theological context and they remain arguments. What they do not remain are Anselm's arguments. For what is central to Anselm's arguments is a conception of God that he derives from his Catholic faith. As an Augustinian, he begins his work by addressing God in prayer and by quoting from the Vulgate reading of Isaiah 7:9, just as Augustine had done. "For I do not seek to understand so that I may believe, but I believe so that I may understand. For I believe this also, that 'unless I believe, I shall not understand'" (*Proslogion* 1).

In what way does faith provide the starting point? By enabling us to conceive of God rightly as he than whom no greater can be conceived. Is God thus conceived a fiction? Does he, as Anselm puts it, exist only in the mind or both in the mind and in reality? Anselm's reply is that God thus conceived *must* exist both in the mind and in reality. Why so? Because, were he not to exist in reality, then we could conceive of a being greater than he, one who did exist both in the mind and in reality. But this would involve us in contradiction, for we would be conceiving of a being greater than the being than whom no greater can be conceived. Hence we must reject the possibility of God, so understood, not existing.

To this another monk, Gaunilo, retorted that, using the same mode of argument, he could prove the existence of a fiction, the so-called Lost Island, an island more excellent than all other islands. For, were we to suppose that this island exists only in the mind and not in reality, then we would be able to conceive of an island with all the excellences of the Lost Island and in addition the excellence of existence, and so we would be conceiving of an island more excellent than the most excellent island of which we conceive. We would have once again contradicted ourselves. But it is absurd to suppose that in this way we can prove the existence of the Lost Island. So Anselm's argument must be rejected.

Three points in Anselm's reply to Gaunilo deserve attention. The first is a distinction that Anselm draws between our conception of God and our conception of any finite being, no matter how perfect. With respect to any finite being of which we can conceive we can conceive of a more excellent finite being of the same kind. There is no upper boundary to the perfections of finite beings. But we conceive of God not as the most excellent of actual beings, one who happens to surpass every other actual being, but as the most excellent conceivable being. It is only because we think of him as such that we cannot think of him as lacking any perfection whatsoever, and therefore it is only to him that we must ascribe existence. The example of the Lost Island or of any other finite being is irrelevant.

Second, Anselm insists on the importance of modal concepts for his argument. If we could conceive of God as possibly not existing, as someone who might have not existed in the past or who might not exist in the future, it would not be God of whom we would be thinking. That is, necessarily we think of God as not possibly not existing, as necessarily existing. Of course, if God cannot not exist, then he exists eternally, for there is no time when he could not have existed. And to think of God as other than eternal would not be to think of God. Gaunilo made the mistake of supposing that Anselm's argument would hold equally of a contingent being, the lost island, and of a necessary being. But it holds only of the latter.

Third, Anselm's chosen antagonist in the *Proslogion* was the Fool, who, according to the psalmist in Psalm 13, has said in his heart "There is no God." But Anselm emphasizes in his reply to Gaunilo that he is no longer arguing with someone foolish, but with someone with whom he shares the Catholic faith. They have therefore in common a conception of God and Anselm is able to appeal to the content of this shared conception in replying to Gaunilo. Does this mean that Anselm's argument can have no purchase on the unbeliever? Does his argument rely on premises that can be affirmed only by believers? This seems to be the case.

When philosophers, whether believing or unbelieving, have rejected Anselm's argument, it has generally been not on account of any misunderstanding, but rather on account of either or both of two features of Anselm's argument that they have understood very well. The first is its treatment of existence as perfection. A being than whom no greater can be conceived must not lack any possible perfection and therefore must be limitless in power, knowledge, and goodness—and must exist in reality as well as in the mind. For, so the argument goes, it is better to exist both in reality and in the mind than only in the mind. But to treat existence as perfection is to treat 'exists' as a predicate and, so it is contended, 'exists' is not a predicate.

What it means to deny that existence is a predicate is easily understood. If I describe some actual or possible finite being, cataloging its qualities, it seems that I can complete that description, whatever the standard of completeness, without saying whether or not this being is indeed actual or only possible, whether or not it exists. Among the predicates that we may use in such descriptions are 'is red,' 'weighs 40 lbs.,' 'is soluble in water,' 'is pear shaped,' 'does the *Times* crossword puzzle regularly,' and 'has a sour taste,' but not 'exists.' The account of existence provided by modern logicians as part of their theory of quantification captures just this distinction between 'exists' and what are taken to be genuine predicates.

To say that unicorns exist is, on this view, to say that something has the property of being a unicorn, that the predication 'is a unicorn' has application to at least one individual. To say that God exists is similarly to say that something is divine. And all claims that something exists are contingent claims, not to be settled by considerations about what is conceivable, so that Anselm's argument must fail.

Is there a response to be made on behalf of Anselm? We might begin by noticing that 'exists' as used by modern quantification theorists can be said equally of numbers and of oak trees. "There is a prime number greater than seventeen and less than twenty-three" and "There is an oak tree in Sherwood Forest" make use of the same 'There is.' But the oak tree, if it exists, has a kind of actuality that the prime number lacks. How are we to express this difference? We might do so by saying of the oak tree, what it makes no sense to say of prime numbers, that it existed at some time between 11:00 and 12:00. When we do so, we use the verb 'to exist' as a verb that has tenses, something not true of the existential quantifier. So of any finite object we may use such predicates as 'used to exist,' 'will exist at some time in the future,' 'exists in the twenty-first century,' 'exists now,' 'began to exist at such and such a time,' 'ceased to exist at such and such a time.'

The predicate ascribing actuality to God is "exists eternally." And the existence that is thus predicated of God is not that of the existential quantifier. But what then is it? It belongs to God necessarily and the unbeliever will at this point reject the concept of a necessarily eternally existing being as incoherent and unintelligible. Invited to respond by demonstrating the coherence and intelligibility of the concept, the Anselmian believer will be un-able to satisfy the unbeliever's demand. Yet this does not give the Anselmian believer reason to judge Anselm's argument unsound. What divides believers from unbelievers at this point is their answer to the question of whether or not the concept of God is the concept of a possible being. Anselm's thesis that necessarily it is true that God exists presupposes that possibly it is true that God exists. But is it? The best arguments that a defender of Anselm can deploy against Anselm's later critics fall far short of showing that the set of predicates ascribed to God can be meaningfully conjoined and ascribed to one and the same being. That they can be so ascribed is a matter of faith, the faith shared by Anselm and Gaunilo, but not by Anselm's more recent critics. So it is indeed the case that for Anselm faith has to precede under-standing. The argument of the *Proslogion* illuminates the philosophical com-mitments of faith. It does not provide grounds for belief for those who would otherwise be unbelievers.

This is not to say that the argument, detached from the context of faith, is not of independent philosophical interest. It has recurrently engaged the at-tention of philosophers of different points of view and even those who have agreed in judging it fallacious have often disagreed on why it is fallacious. What it succeeds in demonstrating to anyone whatsoever, whether theist or atheist, is not the existence of God, but the elusive character of the concept of God, the difficulties that confront someone who wants to deny the exis-tence of God, just as much as they confront anyone who wants to affirm it. And it is an argument whose criticism has been, by any standards, philosoph-ically fruitful. But it was no part of Anselm's intention to contribute to an autonomous secular discipline of philosophy, independent of theology. And, when we write the history of that discipline, and include Anselm's arguments and the debates over those arguments in our narrative, we are assigning to it retrospectively a kind of significance that Anselm himself would not have claimed for it. Using the word "philosopher" as we use it now, we may say of Anselm that he was a philosopher *malgré lui*, as well as the dialectician and the theologian that he took himself to be.

What is true of Anselm is true also of all those who had done their philosophical work in the Augustinian tradition and indeed of their patristic predecessors. In one important way therefore they were not contributing to the Catholic philosophical tradition, that is, to a tradition within which a Catholic allegiance is inseparable from a recognition of philosophical en-quiry as a secular and autonomous activity, a tradition anticipated perhaps only by Boethius. Yet in another way they made a major contribution to that tradition. For, when it finally emerged in the thirteenth century, those who founded it drew heavily on the Augustinian and patristic philosophical resources provided by the theology into which they were educated. So the history of patristic and Augustinian thought is a prologue to the emergence of the Catholic philosophical tradition.

Cited Works by Boethius

Boethius, translations of Aristotle's *De Intepretatione*, *Categories*, the *Prior Analytics*, the *Posterior Analytics*, the *Sophistical Refutations*, and the *Topics*.
Boethius, translations of Porphyry's *Isagōgē*.

Cited Work by Anslem

Proslogion

References

Momigliano, A. "Cassiodorus and the Italian Culture of His Time." *Proceedings of the British Academy* 41 (1955).
Spade, Paul, trans. *Five Texts on the Medieval Problem of Universals*. Indianapolis, IN: Hackett, 1994.
Watts, V. E., trans. "Introduction." *The Consolation of Philosophy*. Harmondsworth, UK: Penguin Books, 1969.

CHAPTER SEVEN

~

The Islamic and Jewish Prologue to Catholic Philosophy

The Catholic philosophical tradition was finally generated when in the thirteenth century what had become the standard Augustinian understanding of the relationship of philosophy to theology was challenged by the rediscovery of Aristotle's texts on physics and biology, on metaphysics and on ethics. The first translations of those texts into Latin were from the Arabic and they were accompanied by translations of Aristotle's Muslim commentators. Those commentators had addressed questions to Aristotle's texts that were in some respects very different from the questions posed by his ancient Greek predecessors and contemporaries. One source of that difference was that, unlike Aristotle, his Muslim readers were theists.

To be a Muslim is to affirm that "there is no god but God and Muhammad is his prophet" and to submit to the will of God. 'Islam' means 'submission.' The God whom Muslims take to speak to them in and through the Qur'ān, those messages believed to have been dictated by an angel to Muhammad, is to be understood as the Creator of the universe, from which he is distinct, as the same God who spoke to Abraham, to Moses, and to Jesus, as one who cares for the needy, and as one who utters a law to which human beings must conform, if they are to receive what they need. Human beings will, after death, be rewarded for submitting to God's will or punished for flouting it. God is the deepest object of human desires and happiness, both in this life and in the life to come, and our happiness is to be achieved only by aligning our will with God's will.

These are not Aristotelian thoughts. What then might the thoughts be of an Islamic reader of Aristotle? The translation of works of Greek science and philosophy into Arabic began within about 120 years after the death of Muhammad in 632. Arab armies had conquered a vast empire for Islam, stretching westward to the Pyrenees, eastward to the borders of India, and northward to the Black and Caspian Seas. Islam was sovereign over large areas whose culture had been first Hellenistic and then Roman. Translators, the majority of them Christians, made available in Arabic a wide range of scientific, medieval, and philosophical works, some translated directly from the Greek, some from Syrian translations of Greek works. In 832 the caliph al-Ma'mūn founded in Baghdad a House of Wisdom (bayt al-ḥikma) where the tasks of translation were systematically pursued and the materials provided for formulating and answering the key questions that arose for Islamic thinkers confronted by Greek philosophy and science. But this was only one source for Islamic philosophical thinking.

The Qur'ān, the traditions regarding the beliefs and practices of Muhammad and his immediate followers (ḥadīth), and Islamic law (sharīa) all required interpretation and interpretation required philosophical reflection. Just as the early Christian theologians found themselves involved in philosophy as part of their theological enterprise, so too did Islamic theologians. Moreover at a relatively early stage, there was a school of Islamic thinkers, the Mu'tazilites, who argued that central Islamic doctrines were justifiable by reason, that God had provided human beings with reason so that they might come to a knowledge of Him, and that the revelation given to Muhammad is consistent with and confirmed by the conclusions of rational enquiry. This was indeed the doctrine adopted and enforced by the caliph al-Ma'mūn, although it was not long before the Mu'tazilite doctrine was rejected and that of the insufficiency of reason to arrive at a knowledge of God reinstated among theologians, especially those under the influence of al-Ash'arï. But debate between various protagonists of these two standpoints continually reemerged, debate that had a certain paradoxical quality.

The air of paradox resulted from the fact that those theologians who defended the view that revelation provided the only knowledge of God and that reason, in the form of philosophical enquiry, was insufficient in all those areas in which revelation was authoritative, found themselves making use of philosophical argument in order to rebut the claims of the philosophers. And, insofar as they were aware of this, they had therefore to distinguish that in philosophy which can serve in the defense of revelation by providing grounds for this rebuttal and that which must be rejected. And in so doing they too became philosophers.

Three areas of conflict between theologians and philosophers were of particular importance. The first concerned the relationship of God to the world. The Qur'ān teaches that God created the world and that there is nothing about each particular human being that escapes God's knowledge. Aristotle held that the world has existed eternally and his account of knowledge makes it problematic as to whether and how God could be acquainted with finite particulars. A second set of issues concerned the relationship of body and soul. The Qur'ān teaches that after the dissolution of the human body the soul survives to be judged by God. Aristotle argued that the soul is a form of the body and the question was therefore raised of how a soul could survive the death of its body. A third set of issues concerned perfected human happiness. Is it achievable in this world, as Aristotle argues, or only in the world to come, as the Qur'ān teaches?

To be a philosopher is not of course necessarily to be in agreement with Aristotle. But it was increasingly an Aristotelian point of view that prevailed among Islamic philosophers and, when the greatest of the Islamic critics of philosophy, al-Ghazālī, attacks philosophers he identifies philosophy with Aristotelian philosophy. The history of Islamic philosophy in the Middle Ages is rich and complex and what I draw from it for my purposes does not even hint at that richness and complexity, for I attend only to philosophers whose texts provided important resources for the Catholic philosophical tradition. So I begin not at or even near the beginning, but with ibn Sīnā (980–1037), educated in Bukhara in the last years of the tenth century. By the age of ten he had memorized the Qur'ān. Before he was eighteen, he had studied the new Arabic arithmetic, Euclid, Ptolemy's *Almagest*, Aristotle's logic, physics, and metaphysics, and finally medicine. He became a physician and the author of the most widely used medical textbook in the Middle Ages from the twelfth century onward, the *Qānūn*, whether in Arabic or in Latin translation. (Ibn Sīnā became known in Christian Europe as Avicenna, a Latinized version of his name used in this translation.) It was in principal part from al-Fārābī's *On the Objects of Metaphysics* that he took his interpretation of Aristotle. But what ibn Sīnā developed out of that interpretation was very much his own and provided a new starting point for enquiry, so that later writers remarkably often define their own positions by their agreements and disagreements with ibn Sīnā.

For ibn Sīnā to explain something is to identify its cause and a cause, as he conceives it, necessitates its effects. But no contingent being acts causally, so as to necessitate its effects. Hence the explanations offered in the particular sciences other than theology are not or not yet genuine explanations. For their enquiries terminate with the operations of contingent beings. To say of a being that it is contingent is to say *both* that it might have had other characteristics than it in fact has and another history than it in fact has *and* that it might not have come to be, that it might not have existed. All finite beings are contingent and, therefore, if we restricted our attention to them, we would have to conclude that the universe might not have existed and there is no contradiction involved in supposing it never to have existed. We need an explanation both of why it exists and of why the finite beings that compose it have the characteristics they have, and have had the history they have had, and no such explanation is complete until it refers us back to the causal activity of a necessary and infinite being. But is there such a being? Ibn Sīnā argues as follows.

What exists must be either necessary or contingent. If it is necessary, then a necessary being exists. If it is contingent, then it must have a cause and that cause must itself be either necessary or contingent. Now there cannot be an infinite sequence of contingent causes—and nothing else. Why not? Ibn Sīnā argues that if there were an infinite set of causes, it would be a self-sustaining complex whole, something dependent on nothing else for its existence. But since its existence would not be contingent on the operation of some other cause that whole would itself be a necessary being. However there cannot be an infinite sequence of contingent causes. For, so ibn Sīnā further argues, if there were an infinite series of causal operations to be traversed before the effect to be explained, namely, the present state of contingent beings, was arrived at, that effect would never be arrived at.

Herbert Davidson has argued that this denial of the possibility of an infinite causal series by ibn Sīnā is unnecessary for his argument (1987, 300–302) and I take him to be right. An infinite sequence of causes and effects, composed only of contingent beings, would itself stand in need of explanation by something other than itself. And since that other must be something that does not itself stand in need of explanation, it must be not only a necessary being, but a necessary being whose necessity is not derived from something else. So, even if ibn Sīnā had been prepared to admit an infinite causal sequence, his premises would still have entailed his conclusion.

Ibn Sīnā goes on to argue that this necessary being must have the unity and the simplicity that characterize God. So his argument becomes an argument to the existence of God. How should we evaluate it? We need to note first of all that ibn Sīnā is committed by his assent to its premises to assert that everything that happens, happens necessarily. What appear to be contingent happenings and states of affairs are in fact necessarily what they are and this is a consequence of the concept of explanation that informs ibn Sīnā's argument. Anyone therefore who insists upon the contingent character of those happenings and states of affairs that are the history of finite beings, whether theist or atheist, is bound to reject some of ibn Sīnā's key premises. Modern atheists however will have a further objection. For they will also argue that to press the demand for explanation beyond the realm of finite beings is to press it illegitimately, that the concepts of cause and explanation find no application beyond the realm of those beings of which we can, at least in principle, become aware in sense experience. Ibn Sīnā himself confronted no atheists. But had he encountered this response, how might he have replied?

He might have suggested that in this respect the burden of proof now falls on the atheists. It is for them to make good on their negative claims. From their standpoint a theist is someone who believes in just one more being than they do and who therefore has the responsibility for justifying her or his belief in this extra entity. But from the standpoint of the theist this is already to have misconceived both God and theistic belief in God. To believe in God is not to believe that in addition to nature, about which atheists and theists can agree, there is something else, about which they disagree. It is rather that theists and atheists disagree about nature as well as about God. For theists believe that nature presents itself as radically incomplete, as requiring a ground beyond itself, if it is to be intelligible, and so their disagreement with atheists involves *everything*. Ibn Sīnā recognized the nature of this disagreement, even though his own argument is one that any orthodox Jewish, Christian, or Islamic theist must reject. For his theism was eccentric. He followed Aristotle in holding that the universe has existed externally—while he rejected the notion of an infinite causal series, he had no difficulty with the notion of an infinite temporal series—and, although his God is not Aristotle's God, like Aristotle's God, ibn Sīnā's God did not preexist the universe.

Ibn Sīnā also followed Aristotle in conceiving of the soul as at once the form that constitutes the matter of the human body as a human body and the principle of the soul's life and activity. It is from the immaterial soul that action originates. Being immaterial, the soul is separable from the body and therefore able to survive the body's death. On the relationship of body to soul ibn Sīnā appears inconsistent. Aristotle was not a dualist and, insofar as ibn Sīnā makes use of Aristotelian concepts of form and matter to elucidate the soul-body relationship, it seems that he too cannot be a dualist. Yet he also uses arguments that commit him to a dualism that is much closer to Plato than to Aristotle and in which indeed, as commentators have pointed out, he anticipates Descartes.

Let someone suppose, ibn Sīnā wrote, that he had just this moment been created, his body floating in air in such a way that he can neither see nor feel any part of that body and so is completely unaware of it. Then ask: Would he affirm his own existence? He would, but in doing so he would be affirming the existence of a self wholly distinct from his body, for he could not affirm the existence of his body. Ibn Sīnā concludes that "the self, whose existence he affirmed, is his distinctive identity, although not identical with his body and his organs, whose existence he did not affirm. Accordingly someone who directs his attention to this consideration has a means of affirming the existence of the soul as something distinct from the body, indeed as something quite other than the body, something that he knows through his own self-awareness" (Shifā', De Anima 1.1, slightly amended from the translation quoted by Goodman, op. cit., p. 156).

This is again very different from Aristotle, of whom ibn Sīnā took himself to be a faithful follower. How did he come to make this mistake? In general ibn Sīnā's predecessors and contemporaries were apt to assimilate Aristotle's thought to that of the Neoplatonists, with the result that they felt free to draw upon Platonic, Neoplatonic, and Aristotelian modes of thought, too often with little or no sense of the tensions or potential conflicts between them. Sometimes the outcome is an inconsistency of which they seem unaware. Yet sometimes it is a creative melding of disparate thoughts. In ibn Sīnā we find both, although often enough he is straightforwardly Aristotelian. He is so most of all in his defense of the various modes of philosophical argument.

In the sixteenth sura of the Qur'ān (16:125) God is represented as commanding Muhammad: "Call human beings into the way of your Lord with wisdom and with fair persuasion and reason with them in the better way." Ibn Sīnā interprets this passage so that the wisdom to which God enjoins his followers is that to be achieved by philosophical demonstration concerning universals, the persuasion that to be achieved by rhetorical argument concerning particulars, and the reasoning with others the reasoning of dialectical argument, through which one criticizes and refutes opposing views. So the Qur'ān summons us, on ibn Sīnā's reading of it, to the enquiries of Aristotle's logic and metaphysics, of Aristotle's rhetoric, and of Aristotle's dialectic.

Yet of course, as we already saw, ibn Sīnā's account of the relationship of God to the world is very different from that of any orthodox reading of the Qur'ān. And this led to a rejection by some Islamic theologians not just of particular positions taken by ibn Sīnā, but of his overall conception of the philosophical enterprise and of its relationship to theology. That rejection received its most notable statement in al-Ghazālī's Tahāfut Al-falāsifa (The Incoherence of the Philosophers). Al-Ghazālī (1058–1111), like ibn Sīnā a Persian—his name was to be Latinized as Algazel—became a student of the theologian al-Juwayni, and, when only thirty-two, was summoned to Baghdad by the vizier of the then sultan to hold a chair in Islamic law. His was the most powerful Islamic mind of his time and—in this like Anselm—he is a major figure in the history of philosophy who never thought of himself as a philosopher. The intellectual tasks he set himself he understood as theological tasks defined by the Qur'ān's teaching of submission to God's will and God's law. External conformity to the precepts of that law is required by God, but he also summons human beings to internalize that law, to submit themselves to him in love and devotion in their interior lives. And it was to this summons to a contemplative life that al-Ghazālī responded when he abandoned his university position, took to the mystical way of the Sufi, and became for ten years a wanderer to Mecca, to Jerusalem, to Damascus, to Hebron, before returning home, where in time he resumed his teaching.

There are two poles to his thought. He is on the one hand concerned to elaborate what it is to be God, as the Qur'ān understands God, and what it is to be a finite being. And he is on the other hand anxious to identify those conclusions of the philosophers that contradict the tenets of orthodox Islamic theology and to show that those conclusions are not supported by sound reasoning. In *The Incoherence of the Philosophers* he examines twenty theses advanced by philosophers, most often by al-Fārābī or ibn Sīnā or both. Of these he takes seventeen to be heretical and three to go beyond heresy into unbelief. Those three doctrines are (1) that the world has existed from all eternity, (2) that God knows only universals and cannot know particulars, and (3) that it is the soul and only the soul that is immortal. The first of these is a denial of the Islamic—and Jewish and Christian—doctrine of creation. The second entails a denial of the Islamic—and Jewish and Christian—doctrine of divine providence. The third is a denial of the Islamic—and Jewish and Christian—doctrine of the resurrection of the body.

Much of what al-Ghazālī rejects in these and other conclusions is Aristotelian. But the Neoplatonic elements in the thought of both al-Fārābī and ibn Sīnā are also at the root of what makes those thinkers problematic for al-Ghazālī. From Neoplatonism ibn Sīnā had taken the view that the world is related to God by way of emanation and that finite beings are necessarily as they are because they come about necessarily. They come about necessarily in virtue of the necessity of God's eternal essence, a necessity he communicates to finite beings. It follows that neither God nor the universe could be other than they are.

From al-Ghazālī's Qur'ānic standpoint this is to misconceive the nature both of God and of finite causality. Notice however that al-Ghazālī does not rest his case on an appeal solely to revelation. He believes as strongly as al-Fārābī and ibn Sīnā that the findings of reason must be consistent with the deliverances of revelation. In the same period in which he wrote *The Incoherence of the Philosophers*, al-Ghazālī also wrote the *Mi'yār al-cilm* (*The Standard for Knowledge*), an exposition of ibn Sīnā's logic. It is to logic that al-Ghazālī appeals in his refutations.

His most general charge against the philosophers—and he equates philosophy with what he understood to be Aristotelian philosophy—is that in their metaphysical thinking they failed to meet the standards to which they were committed by their logic, for they fail to supply conclusive demonstrations of the theses they defend. In consequence of this they disagree among themselves. Moreover the positions they embrace entangle them in contradictions. Consider in this light his criticism of ibn Sīnā's account of causality. Al-Ghazālī has both philosophical and theological objections and they are closely related. According to ibn Sīnā all effects are necessarily the effects of their causes. But, says al-Ghazālī, we have no good reason to ascribe necessity to causal relationships: "The connection between what is habitually believed to be a cause and what is habitually believed to be an effect is not necessary, according to us" (Marmura 1977, 170).

Al-Ghazālī goes on to assert that the only necessary connections of which we know are those that hold between our affirmations and denials and what those affirmations and denials entail. But events in the world are related to other events only by their being conjoined or not conjoined. In cases where observation tells us that they are conjoined, they might not have been. Put cotton in contact with fire and experience tells us that it will burn. But it is always possible that when cotton is put in contact with fire, it will not burn. For al-Ghazālī to say that this is possible is to say no more than that there is no contradiction involved in affirming it. "Possibility" and "necessity" are for him only logical terms.

Theologically this is important because it preserves God's freedom. Al-Ghazālī's most basic theological objection to ibn Sīnā was that his view leaves no place for God as agent, as one who brings about events by his will. From al-Ghazālī's standpoint every event occurs only because God wills it. He is the one true cause. For the most part God's providential ordering of events in the world provides us with the regular sequences—the constant conjunctions—that provide us with our empirical understanding of cause and effect, on which we rely in our practical lives. But at any moment God is free to interrupt those regularities with some miraculous intervention.

Al-Ghazālī's account of causality invited and received a compelling reply from the greatest of all Islamic Aristotelians, ibn Rushd (1126–1198), Latinized as Averroes, author of the *Tahāfut al-tahāfut* (*The Incoherence of the Incoherence*) and of commentaries on Aristotle's *Categories*, *De Interpretatione*,

Topics, Rhetoric, Poetics, De Anima, and *Metaphysics.* Ibn Rushd was born in Cordoba and, until he was seventy years old, lived, taught, and practiced his professions as physician and as Islamic judge in Andalusia. His principal philosophical aims were first to defend Aristotle, as he understood him, and second to show that there was nothing inconsistent in affirming both the truth of Aristotle's conclusions and the truth revealed in the Qur'ān. This however did not make him a defender of all the philosophical theses attacked by al-Ghazālī. For ibn Rushd was on a number of issues philosophically at odds with ibn Sīnā. Concerning the nature of causality ibn Rushd rejected both ibn Sīnā's and al-Ghazālī's accounts.

Like al-Ghazālī, ibn Rushd found ibn Sīnā's claims about causal necessity unacceptable. Ibn Sīnā had represented existence as something conferred on some essences, but not on others, thus making existence an accidental property of those essences. Essences, until existence is conferred upon them, are possibilities. But when existence is so conferred, whatever then exists does so necessarily, a necessity that, as I noted earlier, is transmitted through the causal chains God originates, so that whatever exists, "regarded with respect to its essence, is possible, but, regarded with respect to its actual relation to its causes, is necessary" (Hourani 1974, 14–86).

Against this ibn Rushd argues that existence cannot be an accidental property and that ibn Sīnā has therefore misconceived the relationship of essence and existence. Ibn Rushd follows Aristotle in asserting that only what exists can have either essential or accidental properties. Any notion of essence as somehow prior to existence, so that existence can be conferred upon it, rests on confusions. And the relationships between finite things that exist, substances, are contingent, not necessary. Yet ibn Rushd also rejected al-Ghazālī's conception of causality as a mere regularity about which we have formed habitual expectations. For, were causality what al-Ghazālī takes it to be, all science, all understanding, would be impossible. What then is it to understand?

To understand what something is and why it is as it is, is to understand it in terms of the four types of causality identified by Aristotle: formal, material, efficient, and final. A formal cause is a form in virtue of which this particular something is what it is. Every substance is of some determinate kind, that is, it has properties that are essential to its being of the kind that it is, and to have such properties is to have a specific form. The individual substances that we encounter in perceptual experience are composites of form and matter. Each such individual is, said Aristotle, a "this-such," a "such" by reason of its form, a "this" by reason of the matter in which the form is embodied. And its matter is its material cause. To give the formal cause of something is to answer the question, "What is it?" To give the material cause is to answer the question, "Of what is it composed?" To give the efficient causes is to answer the question, "What agencies brought it about that it is and that it is as it is?" And to give the final cause is to answer the question, "Toward what end is it directed?" So, if the answer to a question about formal causality is "a statue," the answer to the question about material causality might be "bronze," to that about efficient causality "the sculptor," and to that about final causality "to the end of celebrating and commemorating the human being represented." About three of these types of cause something more needs to be said.

First and most obviously if we speak of formal causes as causes, we are not using the word 'cause' as it is used in twenty-first-century languages, where 'cause' is often the equivalent of 'efficient cause.' What then did Aristotle and ibn Rushd mean by 'cause?' For them a cause is that which explains (the Greek word *aitia* and its Arabic equivalent *illat* both mean something that is at once cause and explanation), that which makes intelligible. And in making something intelligible what is primary is the identification of the kind to which it belongs. Matter, as Aristotle and ibn Rushd understood it, is relative to form. The bronze, for example, is matter to which the sculptor has given form. But we can ask about a piece of bronze of what it is composed, treating 'bronze' as the name of the form and whatever the constituents of that bronze are as its matter.

Final causes, the ends to which something is directed by its nature, were in the sixteenth and seventeenth centuries the targets of radical criticism by those who saw belief in them as unscientific superstition. But reference to them has continued to be indispensable in modern biology, where they appear as the ends or functions to the discharge of which a variety of biological systems are directed, as the heart functions in the cardiovascular system to the end that, among other things, the blood may continue to circulate, and also in the explanation of human action.

What is it that these four types of cause render intelligible? The Aristotelian answer is that all of them are indispensable to understanding the changes that the substances we confront in perceptual experience undergo. Those changes take place either accidentally, as when some external force impinges on something, or else as that movement from potentiality to actuality in the course of which things become or fail to become what by their nature they had it in them to become. So acorns become or fail to become oaks and piglets become or fail to become pigs, while, when the growing pig eats the acorn, an accidental cause intervenes to prevent the acorn's further development.

Any movement from potentiality to actuality requires a cause and that cause can effect such a movement only to the extent that it is itself actual. So we begin to make particular changes intelligible by identifying first their immediate causes and then the further causes that produced those causes as their effects. Is there anything to prevent there being an infinite chain of such causes? Aristotle and ibn Rushd agree that there is nothing to prevent this. But if we identify such an infinite series, that there is such a series and that there is this particular series still stand in need of explanation. That explanation can terminate only with a being, not itself a member of the series, which makes it the case that this particular series exists. Such a being must be wholly actual and not itself subject to change. But to be wholly actual such a being must be immaterial. Moreover its existence cannot be contingent upon the activity of some other being, for then it itself would require explanation. So it must be a necessary being, a being that could not have not existed. And this is God.

Thus ibn Rushd has arrived at the same conclusion as ibn Sīnā, but without relying on those theses and concepts to which al-Ghazālī had advanced cogent philosophical objections. His account of necessity and contingency, unlike ibn Sīnā's, does not commit him to understand the entire universe as necessarily being what it is. And his concept of existence is incompatible with ibn Sīnā's thesis that existence is an accidental property of finite beings. What then does ibn Rushd mean by 'exist?' To exist is to be actual. Note that this conception of existence differentiates his view and that of other medieval Aristotelians from the modern view, of which we took note when discussing Anselm's argument, according to which to say that God or volcanoes or numbers exist is to say that something falls under the concept 'God' or the concept 'volcano' or the concept 'number,' that is, the verb 'exists' signifies just as the existential quantifier in logic signifies. So in this modern view God, volcanoes, and numbers all exist in precisely the same sense of 'exist,' but this is not true on ibn Rushd's view.

One important contrast between God and finite beings, on his view, is that no finite being exists necessarily. What it is, its essence, does not in any way entail or imply its existence, which remains surd and unintelligible, until and unless some noncontingent cause of its existence is identified. With God it is otherwise. It is of his essence to exist. It does not follow, as an uncautious reader might think, that therefore Anselm's argument is sound. It would only be sound, if we possess an adequate conception of God's essence, for Anselm's argument begins from how we conceive God. And whether we do indeed possess an adequate conception of God's essence is among those things that are at issue in the debates over Anselm's argument.

Ibn Rushd's defense of philosophical enquiry consisted in a good deal more than a rebuttal of al-Ghazālī's accusations. For he also mounted a theological defense of philosophy, arguing that, if Islamic law is understood rightly, then philosophical activity is a type of activity that the faithful are commanded to undertake. Ibn Rushd quotes from the Qur'ān the injunction to the faithful "Reflect! You have vision" (59:2) and the question posed to unbelievers "Have you not studied the kingdom of the heavens and the earth and whatever things God has created?" (7:185) and interprets them as requiring of human beings a study of the created world guided by the most perfect and complete kind of reasoning, that of demonstrative argument. Demonstrative argument aims at truth and philosophers are those who aspire to discover the truth about the nature of things by rational enquiry. Not every human being is capable of this kind of rational enquiry. Some are capable of being moved to assent only by dialectical arguments, others only by rhetorical persuasion. But there are those who are capable of understanding and of being moved to assent by demonstrative arguments. For this minority the study of ancient authors is required, since it is from them that the relevant philosophy is to be learned. And if anyone were to prohibit those who have sufficient natural intelligence together with the religious integrity and moral virtue necessary for those studies from pursuing them, this would be an act that is "the extreme of ignorance and estrangement from God" (Hourani 1967, 48).

These strong words are important. Ibn Rushd was, like his father and grandfather before him, a judge, and the *Decisive Treatise* was issued as a *fatwa*, a binding pronouncement of law, an adjudication of the case brought against the philosophers by a large number of Islamic theologians, of whom al-Ghazālī had been the most notable. The name that ibn Rushd gives to philosophy is "wisdom," (*ḥikmat*) Aristotle's *sophia*, and he understands the verse in the Qur'ān, "Call human beings to the path of your Lord by wisdom and fair exhortation" (16:125), as enjoining both philosophical argument and religious preaching.

It is not just that the truths of philosophy do not contradict the truths of the Qur'ān. Truth cannot contradict truth, "For truth, as Aristotle says, is consistent and bears witness to itself" (*Long Commentary* 1953, 399). So ibn Rushd concludes that "wherever the conclusion of a demonstration is in conflict with the apparent meaning of Scripture, that apparent meaning admits of allegorical interpretation according to the rules for such interpretation in Arabic" (*Decisive Treatise* 51). The philosopher therefore does more than arrive at certain truths by a different route from that afforded by revelation, since he also contributes to our understanding of the meaning of the texts in which revealed truth is presented (Taylor 2000).

When he was seventy years old, the theological opponents of philosophy in the kingdom where ibn Rushd had been protected by successive rulers had him branded as heterodox and sent into exile. He died at the age of seventy-two. Among his contemporaries the only philosophical writer in Arabic to compare with him was not a Muslim, but a Jew, Mosheh ben Maimon (Mūsā ibn Maimūn in Arabic, Maimonides in Latin) (1135–1204), son of a rabbinical judge in Cordoba. Ben Maimon's family was driven out of Spain by persecution and settled finally in Egypt. Like ibn Sīnā and ibn Rushd, ben Maimon studied medicine, becoming in Cairo a physician to the ruler's vizier. Like ibn Rushd, he was a judge within his own community.

As a Jew ben Maimon is an obedient interpreter of the Torah; as a philosopher he is in general a follower of Aristotle, and a follower also of various Islamic interpreters of Aristotle, especially al-Fārābī and ibn Rushd. As he stated in a letter to Samuel ibn Tibbon: "The works of Aristotle are the roots and foundations of all works on the sciences. But they cannot be understood except with the help of commentaries, those of Alexander of Aphrodisias, those of Themistius, and those of ibn Rushd. I tell you: as for works on logic, one should only study the writings of Abū Nasr al-Fārābī" (Sirat 1985, 161).

Almost all ben Maimon's works were written in Arabic and then translated into Hebrew, and he addressed very different audiences in different works. The *Mishneh Torah*, his codification of biblical and rabbinical statements of divine law, which was written in Hebrew, is addressed to every Jew. *The Guide for the Perplexed* is, by contrast, addressed only to those Jewish readers who have the education and capacity to engage in metaphysical enquiry. The perplexity to be dissolved is that of how to reconcile the authority of scriptural revelation with the truths of the philosophical sciences. This involves learning how what scripture says about God is to be interpreted as well as understanding the conclusions of those sciences. About God we know that he is and what he is not. We know that he is because he revealed himself to the prophets and especially to Moses and because we have a proof that God exists, that he is one, and that he is not a body. The God whose existence is demonstrated is the prime mover of the physical universe as described by Aristotle. Yet, although we know that God exists, we can form no conception of his attributes. It is not just that our conception of them is inadequate, but that the very nature of God, rightly understood, is incompatible with his having attributes. So that whenever we do ascribe attributes to God—and we are authorized by biblical revelation to use certain attributive expressions in speaking of God—we are to understand what we say only as a set of denials, denials that God is limited in the way that we are limited, in respect of his power, goodness, knowledge, and the like.

What we can know of God are his actions. The sciences in teaching us about the created world teach us what God is not. He is one, but not the one of the arithmeticians that can be added and multiplied. He moves the created beings studied by physicists, but he is a mover unlike any physical mover. He reasons, but not as logicians reason. Yet he acts in and through his creation and in knowing his acts we know him. The end to which human beings are directed by their nature is as adequate a knowledge of God as it is possible for them to have. The highest kind of knowledge of God is that of the prophet and only Moses achieved the highest grade of prophetic knowledge. How then may those who aspire to knowledge of God move toward its attainment?

To make knowledge of God one's goal is to set out to remove anything that might come between one and God. To do this is to aim at unqualified obedience to God's will as revealed in his law, the Torah. What kind of human being do we have to become in order to be perfectly obedient? In his commentary on the *Mishnah*, the second century written record of the oral tradition through which divine law is communicated, ben Maimon composed a short treatise on the virtues, the *Shemonah Perakim* (*The Eight Chapters*), in which he adapts Aristotle's account of the moral and intellectual virtues in order to answer this question.

To acquire moral virtue is, as Aristotle says, to have become habituated. "Know that these moral virtues and vices are acquired and firmly established in the soul by frequently repeating the actions pertaining to a particular moral habit over a long period of time and becoming habituated to them. If those actions are good, we shall acquire the virtue; if they are bad, we shall acquire the vice" (Maimon 1975, 68). The precepts of the Torah enjoin just those types of action by the performance of which virtues rather than vices will be acquired. In general ben Maimon follows Aristotle in conceiving of a moral virtue as a norm between two extremes, as, for example, liberality is the mean between extravagance and stinginess, and courage the mean between rashness and cowardliness. Aristotle had nonetheless emphasized that with regard to some traits we are required to move toward one extreme and away from the other, and ben Maimon makes the same point, especially with regard to the putting off of pride and the cultivation of humility. So in a treatise on the laws concerning character traits in the first book of the *Mishneh Torah*, he writes that the good way "is not that a man be merely humble, but that he have a lowly spirit, that he be very submissive. Therefore it was said of Moses our master that he was 'very humble' and not merely humble" (31).

This is of course a biblical and not an Aristotelian view, one quite incompatible with Aristotle's praise of the pride of the magnanimous man (for an extended discussion, see Frank 1989). And it is clear that ben Maimon's use of Aristotle is subordinated to his main purpose, that of elucidating what it is to obey divine law. All human beings are summoned to such obedience, but there is no way of coming to know what that law is apart from God's revelation of it. For although there are certain types of action that humankind in general disapproves as bad, these disapprovals do not themselves have the force of law and there are no "rational laws," laws that unaided human reason can discover (Maimon chap 6). What human beings can achieve without the aid of revelation is a limited agreement on a set of rules founded on these shared disapprovals, rules that may be sufficient to secure some degree of social harmony, so that human beings can live together in political communities, but that do not direct human beings toward their final end, the knowledge and love of God. Only divine law does that.

God revealed his law to the people of Israel through Moses as part of his covenant with them. But earlier in human history, so the Talmud teaches, he had revealed a set of laws binding on all human beings to the descendants of Noah. Six of those laws are prohibitions of: (1) idolatry, (2) blasphemy, (3) murder, (4) adultery, (5) robbery, and (6) the eating of a limb taken from a living animal, while the seventh requires the founding of courts of justice. As with the Mosaic Law, these laws could not be known except by revelation, although we can employ reason to reflect on their purpose and justification. Is it then sufficient for a non-Jew to obey those laws in order to be accounted a righteous Gentile?

Ben Maimon's answer is "No." In the *Mishneh Torah* he wrote: "Any man who accepts the seven commandments and is meticulous in observing them is thereby one of the righteous of the nations of the world, and he has a portion in the world to come." But he immediately added, "This is only the case if he accepts them and observes them because God commanded them in the Torah, and taught us through our teacher, Moses, that the children of Noah were commanded to observe them even before the Torah was given. But if he observes them because of his own conclusions based on reason, then . . . he is not one of the righteous of the nations of the world" (Fox 1972), because he does not obey these laws as laws enacted by God and because they are laws enacted by God.

So ben Maimon, like his Islamic predecessors, puts Aristotelian resources to work in the service of non-Aristotelian purposes. He sees in the moral virtues, as Aristotle describes them, habits that enable human beings to act in accordance with what God's law requires and in the intellectual virtues capacities that enable us to come to know God through obedience to His law. It is insofar as we become perfect in that obedience that we are perfected in our human nature, something impossible for those who understand laws only as precepts that are rationally justifiable because of the social benefits that obedience to them confers.

The Aristotle upon whom ben Maimon draws in arriving at these un-Aristotelian conclusions is of course the Aristotle of his Islamic interpreters, Aristotle rendered from Greek into Arabic. Ben Maimon confronted the same difficulties in being a theistic Aristotelian that his Islamic predecessors had encountered. Is it possible to remain a consistent Aristotelian and to assert that God created the world, that God knows particulars, and that human beings can survive the death of their bodies? Ben Maimon had his own answers to each of these questions, as ibn Sīnā and ibn Rushd had theirs, and the recurrence of the questions reminds us that, although as a Jew ben Maimon's theological enquiries and conclusions were very different from those of Islamic thinkers, as a philosopher he was at work within one and the same tradition of philosophical enquiry. It was part of the greatness of Islamic culture that at certain periods it was hospitable to a kind of philosophical enquiry in which not only Islamic thinkers, but also Jews, Christians, and thinkers who were independent of all three religions, could participate.

Lenn E. Goodman begins his book on *Jewish and Islamic Philosophy* (1999) by telling the story of how shocked a devout Islamic theologian from Andalusia, Abū 'Umar ibn Sa'dī, was by his experience of philosophical debates in Baghdad in the late tenth century, debates in which not only Jews and Christians, but also atheists and materialists—or at least those whom Abū 'Umar took to be atheists and materialists—engaged in argumentative discussions in which appeal to divine revelation was excluded (vii). Yet although in his homeland of Andalusia he might not have found quite the same climate for philosophical discussion, there had been, and would be there too, philosophically fruitful interchanges among Muslims, Jews, and Christians in an atmosphere of intellectual tolerance matched almost nowhere in the medieval Christian world.

In some parts of Spain that fell under Christian rule this tradition continued for considerable periods of time and through it Islamic and Jewish philosophy were transmitted to the Latin Christian world, most importantly, through an impressive sequence of translations. The first great Christian patron of translation in Spain was Raymond, Archbishop of Toledo, from 1126 to 1151. Toledo under Islamic rule had become a city of libraries and it now became a city of translators. We know the names of some major translators into Latin, but it is important that the work of translation was a collective and cooperative rather than an individual enterprise. The language shared by all the translators, Muslim, Jewish, or Christian, was the vernacular, Castilian. Their starting point would be the Arabic text, perhaps some work of Aristotle long before translated first from Greek into Syriac and later from Syriac into Arabic in Baghdad by Syrian Christians, or perhaps some work of one of the Islamic commentators. This would be rendered into Castilian by Jewish or Muslim members of the group of translators and the Castilian would then be translated into Latin, and so Greek and Arabic works became available to the Latin world. But this was not the only way in which or the only place where this happened. In Italy and Sicily a number of Aristotle's works were translated directly from the Greek. Michael Scot (d. ca. 1235), whose popular fame was as a magician, studied at Toledo and translated some Aristotle, some ibn Sīnā, and some ibn Rushd, whence he traveled to Sicily and dedicated his translation of ibn Sīnā to his new patron, Frederick II, Holy Roman Emperor and King of Sicily, himself a speaker and reader of Arabic. It was at Frederick's court that a group of translators, working from the Hebrew translation of ben Maimon's *Guide for the Perplexed* under the direction of Michael Scot, produced a Latin version of that work.

So it was that, by the early thirteenth century, educated people in the Latin West found themselves confronted by a quite new range of texts, some of them key texts of Greek philosophy and science, by Plato, by Aristotle, by Galen, by Ptolemy, some of them texts in which Islamic and Jewish thinkers commented upon and responded to Greek philosophy and science. Their own education in the liberal arts and in theology or law had prepared them for some aspects of this confrontation, but not for others. Unsurprisingly then, there was a range of different and incompatible responses to this new learning and consequent disagreements and conflicts. It was out of those disagreements and conflicts that the Catholic philosophical tradition came to be.

Cited Work by al-Fārābī

Shifā', De Anima

Cited Works by al-Ghazālī

Tahāfut Al-falāsifa (The Incoherence of the Philosophers)
Mi'yār al-cîlm (The Standard for Knowledge)

Cited Works by ibn Rushd (Averroes)

Tahāfut al-tahāfut (The Incoherence of the Incoherence)
Averrois Cordubensis Commentarium Magnum in Aristotelis De Anima Libros (Commentaries on Aristotle's Categories, De Interpretatione, Topics, Rhetoric, Poetics, De Anima, and Metaphysics)
Fasl al-Maqāl (Decisive Treatise)

Cited Works by Mosheh ben Maimon

Mishneh Torah
The Guide for the Perplexed

References

Davidson, Herbert. Proofs for Eternity, Creation, and the Existence of God in Medieval Islamic and Jewish Philosophy. Oxford: Oxford University Press, 1987.
Fox, M., ed. "Maimonides and Aquinas on Natural Law." Diné Israel 3, 1972.
Frank, Daniel H. "Humility as a Virtue: A Maimonidean Critique of Aristotle's Ethics." In Moses Maimonides and His Time. Ed. E. L. Ormsby. Washington, DC: Catholic University of America Press, 1989.
Goodman, Lenn E. Jewish and Islamic Philosophy. Edinburgh: Edinburgh University Press, 1999.
Hourani, G. F. On the Harmony of Religion. London: Luzac & Co., 1967.
Hourani, G. F. "Ibn Sīnā on Necessary and Possible Existence." Philosophical Forum 6, 1974: 14–86.
Long Commentary on the De Anima of Aristotle, Averrois Cordubensis Commentarium Magnum in Aristotelis De Anima Libros, Cambridge, MA: Medieval Academy of America, 1953.
Maimon, Mosheh ben. Eight Chapters. In Ethical Writings of Maimonides. Ed. and trans. C. E. Butterworth and R. L. Weiss. New York: Dover Publications, 1975.
Marmura, M. E., trans. The Incoherence of the Philosophers. Provo, UT: Brigham Young University Press, 1977.
Sirat, Colette. A History of Jewish Philosophy in the Middle Ages. Cambridge, UK: Cambridge University Press, 1985.
Taylor, Richard C. "'Truth does not contradict Truth': Averroes and the Unity of Truth." Topoi 19, 2000.

CHAPTER EIGHT

~

The Genesis of the Catholic
Philosophical Tradition

In all three of the great medieval theistic civilizations, that of Byzantine Christianity, of Islam, and of the Latin West, it is not just that belief in God is so nearly universal that it is, for the most part, taken for granted, but that it is a presupposition of all secular enquiry and activity. To make this or that aspect of the finite world adequately intelligible is to refer it to its relationship to God and the disagreement between theistic and non-theistic cultures is not only a disagreement about God, it is also and perhaps as fundamentally a disagreement about intelligibility. Unsurprisingly then in all three theistic cultures theology is the hegemonic academic discipline, that toward the study of which the secular disciplines are ordered. Nonetheless there were crucial differences between the three cultures in how this ordering was understood.

Among the Byzantines the integration of the imperial bureaucracy and the hierarchy of the church and the subordination of education to their shared purposes was such that anything like a movement toward independent secular enquiry was viewed with immediate suspicion and generally curbed or brought to a halt. It is no accident that no history of modern Western philosophy could be complete that did not include an account of its antecedents in both the Islamic world and the Latin West, yet such a history could safely ignore Byzantine thought, whereas any history of theology would have to take serious account of the Byzantine contribution to it. By contrast, as we have seen, the achievements of philosophy and the sciences in Islamic cultures were notable, although threats to their independence were recurrent from regimes in which, just as in Byzantium, religious and political institutions were integrated. It was as a result of this intolerance that the thought of both ibn Sīnā and ibn Rushd had a continuing afterlife in the Latin West, but not in the Islamic world itself. What then made the Latin West so different from either the Byzantine or the Islamic East?

It was most of all a conception of a need for and the legitimacy of genuinely secular institutions through which God is to be served, of the existence of areas of human activity and enquiry in which the authoritative standards are independent of the authority either of the church or of secular rulers, and this in a way that is in accordance with God's will. This distinctive theistic conception of the autonomy of secular institutions developed through and out of a series of conflicts between rival authorities that involved conflicts about the nature of authority. Some were between secular rulers on the one hand and bishops or popes on the other, others between rival ecclesiastical authorities or rival secular authorities. So alternative and rival answers to questions about the relationship of secular to ecclesiastical authority were posed in political terms that paralleled the competing rival answers to questions debated in the schools about the relationship of secular enquiries to those authoritative teachings to which theologians appealed.

Earlier education in monastic and cathedral schools had been designed primarily, although not only, for those who would proceed beyond the seven liberal arts to the study of theology. But from the early twelfth century onward both teachers and students in the liberal arts had increasingly secular preoccupations. When I speak of the preoccupations of students and teachers as secular, I do not mean by this only that the ambitions of many of the students were secular ambitions. More important is the fact that each of the liberal arts was understood as contributing to an integrated body of secular knowledge. That understanding was sometimes expressed in charts of the tree of knowledge in which the knowledge of nature and of human nature is represented as an autonomous or semiautonomous realm. It is not that the teachers in the schools did not recognize that theology affords us knowledge of a higher order. Abelard, Hugh of St. Victor, William of Conches, and Thierry of Chartres were theologians as well as teachers of logic, dialectic, and natural science. Indeed Abelard's primary interest in logic was to throw light on the mystery of the Holy Trinity.

Moreover we should not exaggerate discontinuities with past teaching. The theology of these new teachers remained Augustinian, although their philosophy was heavily influenced by the Platonism that had been transmitted to them, partly through Augustine, partly from Neoplatonic sources, partly through Boethius, who was also the source of that in Aristotle of which they were aware. But they also knew something of ancient atomism—William of Conches was an atomist—and something of Stoicism. Yet they were moved by a new desire to give a systematic account of everything known within a single framework and with it there developed an equally new sense that theologians needed knowledge of the natural and the historical world, if they were to do their own theological work adequately.

What they lacked were adequate means to enlarge their knowledge of the natural and the historical. What they therefore practiced were modes of enquiry that would later on be put to uses of which they themselves could not as yet conceive. Three of those contributions to modes of enquiry became permanently important. The first was the development of the *quaestio*. *Quaestiones*, questions about alternative interpretations of a passage in scripture or its implications, had begun in the eleventh century to play an increasing part in commentaries on scripture. A statement of a question is followed by alternative answers to it and a summary of arguments in favor of and against each answer. Out of this develops a notion of enquiry as constituted by an unfolding sequence of *quaestiones*, directed toward a perfected understanding of the subject-matter of those questions and answers.

Second, there was an increasingly sophisticated use of dialectic as a means of resolving problems posed by rival solutions to such questions. What the dialectician aims to do, following Aristotle and Boethius, is to argue from premises accepted by those with whom he is in controversy, so as to arrive at truths that will withstand objections from any point of view, and so finally at first principles from which demonstrative argument may proceed. A sequence of *quaestiones*, the responses to which make use of dialectic, so understood, may thus become a means to the construction of a demonstrative science. But the construction of such a science in any particular field will have to rely heavily on those texts that at that time are honored as authoritative in that field. What then is it in the twelfth century for a text to be treated as authoritative? An authoritative text is one whose theses and arguments have so far withstood refutation. Holy Scripture is authoritative because God speaks in and through its texts, so that they are not open to refutation. But Holy Scripture, just like secular texts, stands in need of interpretation and the third great achievement of the schools of the twelfth century, alongside those of the *quaestio* as a mode of enquiry and of the use of dialectic, was to develop more systematically than previously an account of the different senses that a passage in a text might have. Moreover, the making of *distinctiones* with respect to the sense of a given thesis provided dialecticians with further material for their arguments and so enabled them to provide more compelling accounts of those inconsistencies and incompatibilities that generate problems both in theology and in the liberal arts.

What the teachers of the twelfth century schools retained from their predecessors was a conception of dialectical enquiry as subordinated to their theological commitments, and along with it a view of the curriculum as structured by theology, the seven liberal arts, and the mechanical or useful arts. Where they innovated or learned new truths from external sources, they were able to accommodate what they had discovered or learned within this established framework. And before that framework was challenged by the rediscovery of Aristotle's natural science, metaphysics, and ethics, the institutions within which such teachers did their work had already been transformed, as the first universities came into being. How this happened differed from place to place. There is one story to be told about Paris, another about Bologna, a third about Naples. But there are three strands common to all these stories. One is a strengthening of the sense of a common professional identity among masters who were teaching various disciplines in various types of school. Teachers of theology, of the liberal arts, of law, and of medicine increasingly were able to recognize each other as colleagues with the same professional values.

A second strand is the increasing centralization of authority and power in both church and secular government. Emperors and kings imposed a rule of law and systems of law courts and taxation. Local customs and local authority were more or less—often less—effectively subordinated to central power. And so it was too with popes and bishops. Innocent III encouraged the settlement of local disputes at local levels, but thereby Rome became a more effective final court of appeal, and bishops were now required to give an account of themselves at Rome every four years. The Fourth Lateran Council in 1215 was the culmination of Innocent's administrative reformation of the Catholic Church in which older rules were enforced and new rules imposed. These changing structures of both church and secular government required a more highly educated clergy and laity than before. And so the reorganization of education by teachers in emerging universities invited and received the patronage of popes, bishops, emperors, and kings. Correspondingly—and this is a third strand—there was a steady growth in student demand for instruction in the liberal arts, in theology, and in law. New opportunities opened up for the ambitious and those opportunities were available only for those with the requisite education. So cities in which universities were founded had to accommodate an influx of the young and often disorderly, and so trades such as book copying and bookselling flourished.

The relative importance of each of these three strands varied from place to place. At Bologna, as later at Glasgow, the university emerged in response to student demand and the students ruled their university through a lord rector whom they elected. The masters were in effect the employees of the students. Unsurprisingly the study of law had chief place in their curriculum. The University of Naples by contrast came into existence in 1224 at the fiat of Frederick II, to serve his purposes as ruler of his kingdom of Sicily. His subjects were forbidden to study or teach elsewhere and the curriculum was designed to provide his government with skilled manpower. The chief place was given to law and medicine (nearby Salerno was already a famed medical school), the liberal arts were a prologue to these professional studies, and, while some theology was taught, it was the least flourishing of the disciplines.

The University of Paris, unlike either Bologna or Naples, was a university in which the masters ruled. Their authority over the affairs of the university had been established by appeal to the pope. At Paris theology was the hegemonic discipline and all seven liberal arts—grammar, rhetoric, logic, arithmetic, music, geometry, and astronomy—were taught, as were law and medicine. But the majority of students did not progress beyond the liberal arts.

It is of course anachronistic to use the word "university" of Paris or Naples or Bologna or any other academic institution in the twelfth and thirteenth centuries. What we have been calling a university was a *studium* or, more precisely, a *studium generale*, although these names were also used of other types of institution, such as the houses of study of the Dominican order. The concept of a university finds fully fledged application only later, at the end of the thirteenth century, when there is mutual recognition by universities of their distinctive function and status, a recognition signaled by an acknowledgement, at least in theory, that a master's degree from any university conferred the *ius ubique docendi*, the right of teaching anywhere.

Yet of course this prosaic history only has the far from prosaic significance that it has because of what it was that was taught and the conflicts that resulted. It was because thirteenth-century European universities, developing out of conjunctions of the academic ambitions of masters, the desire for increased power by rulers, and the striving for upward mobility by students, became scenes of intellectual conflict, places where the fundamental issues that divided and defined the age were articulated, that their history provides the setting for the emergence of the Catholic philosophical tradition. What the teachers in the earlier schools had provided, through their uses of the quaestio and of dialectic, was a method of formulating and, if possible resolving, more or less radical disagreements. What the setting of the university now provided was a milieu within which the statement and resolution of fundamental disagreements within the disciplines and between the disciplines were given institutional form. And it was as the first great universities came into being that intellectual conflicts of a fundamental kind became inescapable. So what happened in universities and especially in the University of Paris became of great importance for the culture as a whole.

The statutes of the University of Paris enacted in 1215 repeated a prohibition that had been in force since 1210, forbidding the teaching of Aristotle's works of natural science and metaphysics, or of commentaries upon them, by masters of the arts faculty. This proscription remained in force for more than twenty years, but gradually fell into abeyance until in 1255 the faculty of arts at Paris adopted a new curriculum, one that prescribed the teaching of Aristotle's entire works. What was at stake in the prohibition and in its reversal?

The translation of those works of Aristotle hitherto unknown in the Latin West, first from Arabic and then from Greek during the twelfth and thirteenth centuries, enlarged and transformed the conception of secular knowledge shared by the educated and with it all those issues concerning the relationship of secular knowledge to theology that had hitherto been dealt with from within an Augustinian framework. Aristotle, understood in the light afforded by his Islamic commentators, provided a new and systematic account of what it is to understand the natural world and the human mind's engagement with it, an account at once deeply compelling and yet apparently at key points at odds with Christian belief. Why was it compelling? Partly, because at that time and place, it had no rival.

Thirteenth-century readers of Aristotle learned from his writings about a variety of types of enquiry and understanding undertaken by his predecessors and contemporaries, by a variety of pre-Socratic philosophers, by Plato, and by some of Plato's other students. In each case Aristotle identified what he took to be the limitations of that mode of enquiry and claimed to be able to integrate what was of value into his own projects of enquiry and understanding. And, insofar as twelfth- and thirteenth-century readers found these claims compelling, they had every reason to identify themselves with Aristotle's projects. Moreover they had before them the examples of those Islamic and Jewish thinkers who had already found reason to accept Aristotle's central claims. So the question of the relationship of philosophy to theology became the question of the relationship of Aristotle's philosophy—and science—to theology.

Many Augustinian theologians found what they took to be good reason to reject both Aristotelianism itself and the Aristotelian claim that philosophical enquiry has its own standards and methods, independent of those of theology. Some of them were prepared in the course of their theological enquiries to appeal to this or that particular Aristotelian thesis or argument. But they resisted the central claims made by the new Aristotelians for the same reasons that Islamic theologians had done, although not only for these. They followed their Islamic predecessors in taking Aristotle's doctrine of the eternity of the universe, his account of the relationship of soul and body, and his conception of human happiness and how it is to be achieved to provide sufficient grounds for Christians to reject any type of Aristotelianism. But ibn Rushd and his followers had provided them with an additional reason. Of Aristotle, ibn Rushd had written in a commentary on the *De Anima* that he was "the exemplar that nature found to reveal the ultimate in human perfection." And it did indeed seem that on an Averroistic Aristotelian view the highest human achievements are those of the speculative intelligence. Yet for a Catholic Christian it is in Jesus Christ alone that we are able to see humanity perfected. And this by itself would have provided sufficient reason for Augustinian Christians to reject Averroism.

One response to this rejection by some Averroistic Aristotelians in the University of Paris was to propound a doctrine of two truths. Aristotle, as understood by Averroes, and Catholic Christian doctrine do indeed, they conceded, appear to be incompatible, just as the Augustinians claim. That is, it seems that if certain Aristotelian theses are true, then some Christian doctrines are false and vice versa. But this seems to be so only because of the misleading view that there is a single concept of truth—and this is not so. What is affirmed as true in one domain of enquiry may be affirmed as false in another without any inconsistency. So it may be true in philosophy and by the standards appropriate to philosophy that the universe is uncreated and has existed eternally, while it is true in theology and by the standards appropriate to theology that the universe was created by God and has only existed for a certain period of time. In philosophy as an Averroistic Aristotelian I may assert that the universe has existed eternally, yet as a Catholic Christian I continue without inconsistency to say and believe the creeds.

This Averroistic view of truth, which Aquinas both expounded and refuted, involves three large and closely related mistakes. A first concerns the predicate "is true" and its indispensable function in discourse. To make any assertion whatsoever is to be committed to the judgment that that assertion is true—not true in this or that domain, not true for this or that group of human beings, but true. For, if I first assert that p and subsequently deny that p is true, I am withdrawing my initial assertion. And if I assert that p and stand by my assertion, then I am committed to denying the truth of *any* assertion incompatible with p, no matter in what domain or by what standards it is asserted.

Second, incompatibility between assertions is inseparable from their having the meaningful content that they do. The meaning of "The universe has existed eternally" is such that anyone who asserts that sentence has thereby denied that the universe has existed only for a certain period of time. Someone who has not grasped this has failed to understand the meaning of the sentence "The universe has existed eternally." And someone who attempts, as some Averroists seem to have done, to assert both that the universe has existed eternally *and* that it has existed only for a certain period of time, even if he makes the first assertion qua philosopher and the second qua theologian, has made it quite unclear what he could have meant by either assertion.

Third, there are indeed different and distinct domains of enquiry, each with its own standards for distinguishing the true from the false. Mathematics is one such domain, physics another, history a third, theology a fourth. But these domains are not self-enclosed, so that the truths in any one domain have no implications for what is true or false in any of the others. Some truths in physics exclude certain historical possibilities. Some truths in mathematics exclude certain physical possibilities. Some truths in theology exclude certain physical and certain philosophical possibilities. So the attempt by some Averroists to insulate theology from philosophy and the natural sciences could not but fail. That it did in fact fail was to be demonstrated by Aquinas, invoking just the kind of consideration that I have outlined.

Aquinas's refutation of the Averroist view was important not only for the future history of philosophy, but also for the future history of universities. The schools that were the predecessors of universities had been primarily places of teaching and only secondarily and, on occasion, places of enquiry. But even in them it had been becoming clear that teaching, which is to succeed in making the resources of past learning available in the present, is inseparable from ongoing enquiry, from reformulating old questions, testing established beliefs, asking new questions, and so providing new resources for teaching. With the establishment of universities this relationship between teaching and enquiry becomes institutionalized. For both teaching and enquiry an adequate grasp of the concept of truth is crucial for at least three reasons.

First, the attainment of truth is integral to the goal of understanding. Acts of understanding always involve knowledge of truths and of the relationship of those truths to others. Second, insofar as the achievement of a perfected understanding of the nature of things requires relating the truths of theology to those of a variety of other disciplines, it matters not only that within each discipline enquirers acknowledge the various standards by which truth is discriminated from falsity, but also that they share a single concept of truth that gives point and purpose to the application of those standards. Third and finally, the project of understanding is not one only for those engaged in teaching, studying, and enquiring within universities. Every one of us, in our everyday lives, needs in a variety of ways to learn and to understand. The ability of those outside universities to learn and to understand what they need to learn can be helped or hindered by the good or bad effects on their intellectual formation and their thinking of those who have been educated in universities, by the good or bad influence, that is, not only of parents, but also of school teachers, pastors, and others. One condition for that influence being good rather than bad is that what is communicated to and shared by the whole community of teachers and learners is a respect for truth and a grasp of truths that presupposes, even if it is never or rarely explicitly spelled out, an adequate conception of truth. One of our debts to Aquinas is that he, both in his own account of truth and in his disputes with the Averroists, taught us to appreciate this.

AQUINAS AND AFTER

CHAPTER NINE

~

Aquinas: Philosophy and Our Knowledge of God

Tomasso di Aquino, Thomas Aquinas, a Dominican friar, was already deeply committed to both Augustinian theology and Aristotelian philosophy when, at around the age of thirty-one, he became a regent master in the University of Paris in 1256. His academic career had begun four years earlier when he started teaching the basic theological text, Peter Lombard's *Sentences*. Before that he had been a student of Albertus Magnus, whose theological writings and commentaries on Aristotle show him to have been the ideal teacher for anyone who wished to understand both Augustinian theology and Aristotelian philosophy. But Albertus himself left open the question of what the relationship between them is or should be.

Aquinas understood from the outset that clarity about the nature of that relationship required an understanding of the concepts that are either used or presupposed in both areas of enquiry. Even before he became a regent master he had written a short but seminal treatise, the *De Ente et Essentia*, in which he drew upon Avicennas's thought as well as Aristotle's, but put what he learned from them to original uses. Aquinas follows Aristotle in distinguishing two senses of 'a being,' in Aquinas's Latin *ens*, one in which we may say of anything about which we can make true assertions that it is, that it is a being—this is the 'is' of the existential quantifier in modern logic—the other in which by asserting that something is, that it is a being, we assert that it is actual. It is of the latter that we ask and answer the questions: "What is it?" "What are its essential properties, its essence?"

The *entia* that we encounter in perceptual experience are composites of form and matter. Different particulars may have the same form—as human beings, as wolves, as trees, as stars—and so belong to the same species, but are different individuals just because they differ in their matter. Essence, *essentia*, signifies what this or that particular composite of matter and form is. Of any substance therefore we can assert that it is and enquire what it is. Moreover our knowledge of what some kind of thing is may be independent of our knowledge that it is. We can understand what a human being is or what a phoenix is without knowing whether or not there is such a being. Therefore that some particular substance is is something other than and over above what it is. Its *esse*, its act of existing, is other than its nature, its essentia. So I can only understand a substance as a possibility made actual by existence having been conferred upon its essence. But this presupposes some source of existence, some being whose being is not to be understood either as a composite of form and matter or as one in whom essence and existence are distinct, but as a being whose essentia is his esse, God. Note that we are not to think of essences as somehow preexisting, waiting for existence to be conferred on them. Nonetheless essence is to be distinguished both conceptually and really from existence.

The detail of Aquinas's arguments is important. By providing accounts of how essence is related to definition, to genus and species, to substance and to accident, and to composite and noncomposite beings, he does two things. He elucidates what he takes to be presupposed by our everyday discourse and enquiries about beings and being and he provides a vocabulary for further enquiry, a vocabulary that is put to use throughout his subsequent work.

Before he left the University of Paris for Italy in 1260 Aquinas had begun work on his *Summa contra Gentiles*. The gentiles of the title are those pagan thinkers who, not having encountered God's self-revelation to Israel and in Jesus Christ, had reasoned their way to a variety of conclusions about the nature of things. Aquinas's project is that of showing how, rightly understood, the philosophical enquiries in which they had engaged arrive at conclusions that are not only congruent with, but direct us toward the truths of the Christian revelation. At the beginning of book 2 of the *Summa contra Gentiles*, written while Aquinas was at work in Italy, almost certainly in the Dominican house in Naples, he considered the difference between philosophical and theological enquiries.

Philosophy begins from finite things as they are and from what belongs to them by nature. It leads us from them through an enquiry into their proper causes to knowledge of God. Theology by contrast begins from God and considers finite beings only in their relationship to God. So, although there are matters of which theology treats and philosophy does not and vice versa, they also have a common subject matter. Aquinas's claim is not just that theology and philosophy must be consistent—on this his treatment of truth is decisive—but also that failure to understand the universe of finite created beings inevitably issues in a defective knowledge of God. Why so?

We understand God as creator in part through a study of the natural order of things and of the human place within that order. Errors about that order and about the human place within it give rise to errors about God himself and our relationship to him. So that philosophy and the natural sciences are required as a complement to theology, as more than a rational prologue to it. Yet, if this is so, it is all the more important to correct errors perpetuated by those engaged in philosophical and scientific enquiries, among them the errors of those who suppose that a commitment to Aristotelianism necessitates a denial that the world has existed for a finite time, that perfected human happiness can only be achieved in the world to come and that the human soul does not survive the death of the body.

Aquinas's philosophical commitment to Aristotelianism was almost, if not quite unqualified. His early education at the University of Naples had introduced him to Aristotle's scientific texts at a time when they were not yet taught in the University of Paris. His reference to Aristotle as "the philosopher"—and indeed to Averroes as "the commentator"—makes evident his identification of the cause of philosophy with the cause of Aristotle. Unsurprisingly, some Franciscan Augustinians, deeply critical of Averroist Aristotelianism, mistakenly treated Aquinas as just one more Latin Averroist. Aquinas had however developed a set of distinctive positions with regard to the central disputed issues.

On the eternity of the world he argued that both the arguments advanced by Aristotle in favor of this thesis and the arguments that can be advanced against Aristotle's view are inconclusive. This is a question that cannot be decided by the power of natural reason and therefore when, on the basis of revelation, Christians affirm the doctrine of creation they contradict no defensible thesis of philosophy or science. About human happiness Aquinas argued that there is indeed genuine happiness to be achieved in this present world, a kind of happiness that is well worth achieving, but that nonetheless it is always imperfect happiness. Even if achieved, it leaves the natural desire of human beings for perfected happiness unsatisfied. Aquinas argues that no finite object or state of affairs could be such as to satisfy that desire. To this point reason in the form of philosophical enquiry can take us. About the nature of that vision of and friendship with God in which alone is to be found perfected happiness only God's self-revelation, to be apprehended by faith through a life of hope and charity, can inform us.

In so arguing Aquinas highlights two contrasts, one intentionally, one perhaps unintentionally. The first is that between the limits of philosophical understanding and what reflective theological enquiry, appealing to truths of revelation, can disclose to us. Although Aquinas as both theologian and philosopher moves easily between them, he is always alert to the distinction. Although he is unflinchingly Augustinian in his theology, he treats philosophy as an independent form of enquiry in a way and to a degree that Augustine never did. A second contrast is between the standpoint of the theist and that of the atheist. With the latter Aquinas is not explicitly concerned. He recognized that "human reason is deficient in matters concerning God," that, if our only knowledge of God were that at which we arrive by reasoning, many individuals would never attain any knowledge of God, and that philosophers have recurrently fallen into error and disagreed among themselves (*Summa Theologiae* II–IIae 2.4). He had catalogued what he took to be the most powerful objections to the assertion of God's existence before setting out each of the five ways by which he believed that divine existence can be demonstrated. But, unlike us, he did not inhabit a culture in which arguments for the denial of God's existence have been advanced for hundreds of years and in which that denial has become commonplace. So that we here now are far better placed than Aquinas was to ask what it is that distinguishes Aquinas's theistic standpoint for the standpoint of the atheist, what it is that is most basic in their disagreement.

To this it may be retorted that the answer is obvious. The disagreement is as to whether God does or does not exist. But this retort misses the point, for the disagreement between atheists and theists is one of those fundamental disagreements that extends to how the disagreement is to be characterized. Atheists characteristically take theists to believe in one item too many. They envisage a catalog designed to include a description of every type of being that there is and suppose that theists and atheists have no problem in agreeing to include in that catalog a variety of inorganic and organic beings, stars, planets, dandelions, azaleas, bacteria, viruses, dolphins, wolves, and the like, but disagree about just one remaining item, God. And since none of the reasons that are sufficient to justify the inclusion of descriptions of all these other beings are sufficient to justify the inclusion of a description of God, they take it that theists have at this point affirmed a belief which, unlike those beliefs that theists and atheists share, lacks rational justification. The atheist has, on the atheist's view, conformed to the canons of rationality. The theist has not.

This is not however how theists characteristically understand their disagreement with atheists. From the theistic point of view this is a disagreement about everything, about what it is to find anything whatsoever intelligible rather than unintelligible. To view something as intelligible is not yet to understand it. It is to recognize it as open to being understood, to recognize that, if one asks what it is, why it is as it is, and why indeed it is—why, that is, out of the indefinitely large set of possibilities that might have been actualized, this particular possibility has been realized—there is a true answer to be found. That answer will identify some agency sufficient to make it the case that things exist as they do and have the characteristics that they have.

It turns out however that no answer provided by the natural sciences is capable of identifying such an agency. For all scientific explanation is of the form "Because such and such antecedent conditions were satisfied, these particular possibilities were actualized" and this makes the outcome that we are trying to understand intelligible only if we are able to say why those particular antecedent conditions were satisfied. No matter how far scientific explanation is taken, the existence of whatever it is that exists and its having the characteristics that it has remain surd facts, yet to be made intelligible. And this is why scientific enquiry always involves trying to move beyond our present explanations, yet never can reach a point where the phenomena that it studies have been made finally intelligible. What kind of agency would have to be identified to make them finally intelligible? It would have to be such that it itself, its existence and nature, require no further explanation, that is, that there is no question of existence having been conferred on its essence, something ruled out only if *what it is* and *that it is* are one and the same, that it is a being whose essence and existence are identical. But this is how theists conceive of God. So their disagreements with atheists concerning God are inseparable from their disagreements with atheists concerning intelligibility—and these disagreements have a further dimension.

What is distinctive about the theistic view of the nature of things is not only that theists assert the existence of God and that they take the world to be fully intelligible only if understood in its relationship to God, but that they conceive of human beings as occupying a unique position in the order of things. Human beings are on the one hand bodies, having a physical, chemical, and animal nature, inhabiting an immediate environment, located at particular points in space and time. Yet on the other hand their understanding extends indefinitely beyond their immediate environment to what is remote in space and time and to the abstract and the universal as well as to the concrete and the particular. And their aspiration to complete and perfect their understanding of the order of things and of their place within it is matched by an aspiration to achieve a relationship with a fully and finally adequate object of desire, an end to which, if they understand themselves rightly (on the theistic view), they are directed by their nature. Yet human beings are not animal bodies plus something else. The human being is a unity, not a duality.

This theistic view of human beings stands in sharp contrast to two rival views. One is the Platonic view of the human being according to which the soul, that in us that thinks, desires, and wills is one thing, the body quite another. There have been different versions of Platonism, the best worked out and most compellingly argued of which is that, advanced by Plotinus, some aspects of which I outlined in chapter 4. On any Platonic view I *have*—in this present life at least—a body, but I *am* my soul, and my continuing identity as a soul will be unaffected by the death and dissolution of my body. Indeed for Plato and Plotinus, although not for Christian Platonists, I existed as a soul before I acquired a body. And for Plato and Plotinus, although once again not for Christian Platonists, the body imprisons the soul and death is to be welcomed as a liberation from the body.

Sharply contrasted with this Platonic conception of the human being is the materialist conception, presented successively in the ancient world by such thinkers as Leucippus, Democritus, Epicurus, and Lucretius, according to which nothing exists that is not a body and human beings just are their bodies. The human mind and soul are no other than and no more than modes of functioning of the human body. I did not preexist the existence of my body and I will not exist after my body's death and dissolution. My thoughts and my desires are somehow or other reducible to and explicable in terms of my bodily states and processes. Materialism, like Platonism, has had a number of significantly different versions, the most sophisticated of which were not advanced until the twentieth century. But the versions of both Platonism and materialism of which Aquinas was aware enabled him to identify and discuss the crucial issues that each raises.

Insofar as Platonism was influential in the thirteenth century, it was so because of Plato's and Plotinus's influence on Augustine. But Aquinas was always careful not to assimilate Augustine's views to Plato's too closely—he, a non-Platonist, regarded himself as a faithful follower of Augustine—and he addressed Plato's views directly and not only in the form that they had taken on in the thirteenth century. Materialism's importance for him was not just a matter of those arguments advanced by its ancient exponents, but also of the problems posed by ibn Rushd's interpretation of Aristotle, as it was presented by the Latin Averroists. What, on Aristotle's view, was mistaken in materialism was its assumption that by identifying the elements out of which some body was constructed, one had answered the questions: What is it? What is its nature? Living bodies are unities, not just collections of material elements. And what kind of unity a particular living body has is a matter of its specific form. Withdraw the unity conferring form from a living body and it is no longer a living body, but only a collection of material elements.

In early Greek thought the name given to whatever it is that is present in a living body, but absent from a dead one was *psychē*, which was later translated by the Latin *anima* and by the English *soul*. Aristotle therefore takes the form of a living body to be its *psychē*, its soul. The soul is thus not something over and above the living body. It constitutes the living body as the kind of living body that it is with the kind of powers that it has. And so it is with the bodies of human beings, members of the species *rational animal*. The human soul is the form of the human body. Withdraw the soul and what is left is no longer a living, let alone a human, body. The human soul is not the human mind. To speak of the mind is to speak of the intellectual powers that human beings have in virtue of their specific nature. But what is it then that happens to a human being at the moment of death?

The matter that was her or his matter is no longer unified by form. And, since it may seem that form has no reality except as informing matter, whatever it was that existed as matter unified by form no longer exists. What was a human being, a human body, now lacks a soul and what might soul without body be? The question could not be evaded by any convinced Aristotelian and Aquinas was a convinced Aristotelian, committed to thinking about living bodies, and therefore about human bodies, in just the terms in which Aristotle had thought about them. He therefore had the same problem that ibn Rushd and the Latin Averroists had had, that of reconciling his theological belief that the human being survives death and after death is judged by God with his Aristotelian philosophical commitments.

Aristotle had however argued that, while perception is dependent on and affected by the bodily sense organs through which it perceives, the intellect is not thus dependent, but is separated from the body (*De Anima* 429b 4–5). Aristotle's own further development of this thesis had been interpreted differently by different commentators, including ibn Rushd, whose philosophical conclusion seemed to be that, even if, in some way and some sense, thought was independent of body and imperishable, nonetheless what survived death was not the individual human being. Yet ibn Rushd, as a devout Moslem, believed that individual human beings do survive their death and he seems to have envisaged this as a resurrection of the body. Aquinas by contrast moved from this thesis of Aristotle in a very different direction.

The question that Aquinas poses in the *Quaestiones Disputatae de Anima* is whether the human soul can be both a form and a particular, a this-something, a thing (*tode ti* in Aristotle's Greek, *hoc aliquid* in Aquinas's Latin; I shall follow Timothy McDermott (1993), who translates Aquinas's question as "Can the human soul be both a form and itself a thing?" [184]). It seems, so Aquinas replies, that nothing can be at once a form and itself a thing. And indeed, if the soul were itself a thing, it seems that it could not stand to its body as a form stands to a body. And Aquinas proceeds further by considering a number of versions of these difficulties, in the course of which he concludes that, if any thing is itself a thing, "then it must have its own activity peculiar to it, since everything that exists in its own right has its own activity" (art. I, *Quaestiones Disputatae de Anima* in McDermott 1993, 185). Aquinas then considers what a form is. It is that which confers on a body whatever it is that constitutes the specific nature of that body. What is the specific nature of a human body? It is, as we just noted, the body of a rational animal and one essential characteristic of a rational animal is that it should have the power to think and, by thinking, to understand. So the form that constitutes a body a human body, that is, its soul, must be that in virtue of which it has the power to think and to understand. But, if this is so, then the soul does have its own peculiar activity, that of thinking and, by thinking, achieving understanding.

We might be misled into supposing otherwise by recognizing that human beings are only able to exercise their intellectual powers because they also have perceptual powers. It is only from what we perceive and as a result of what we perceive that we acquire the concepts that provide our thought with its subject matter. But, since sense perception could not occur without sensory organs, that is, without a body, each human mind is dependent on its body. Without its body it would have nothing to think about and nothing to think. What matters, however, according to Aquinas, is that once we have been furnished with something to think about and the means to think about it, the activity of thinking informed by the goal of perfected understanding becomes independent of the body, able to free itself from dependence on its bodily expressions, and needing no part of the body as its instrument, I see with my eyes, I pick things up with my hands, I think with. . . ? It is Aquinas's claim that for thinking nothing plays the part that the eyes play in seeing or that the hands play in picking things up.

Many contemporary readers will at this point exclaim indignantly: "But of course I think with something! I think with my brain!" What has to be said to such readers? That they are making an inference from the premise "Whenever in our present life thought occurs, observable changes occur in some region of the brain" to the conclusion "Just as we see with our eyes, so we think with our brains." Their premise is certainly true and the evidence for its truth is impressive. But it provides us with no good reasons for making that inference. The characteristic contemporary response to this denial is to provide yet further evidence for the truth of the premise by listing those neurophysiological and biochemical discoveries that have made recent investigations of the brain so rewarding. But this response is not to the point. Something more than evidence for the truth of the premise is needed, if the inference is to be warranted, and nothing more has been provided.

Yet, if we can successfully defend Aquinas in this way, another difficulty arises. If the activity of thought can indeed be independent of the body, as Aquinas claims, then thought must have the characteristics that Plotinus ascribed to it, the characteristics that make it impossible to identify intellectual activity with bodily states and processes. But in that case how is Aquinas to distinguish his position from that of the Platonists? Aquinas has an insightful answer.

What makes this particular thought that I am now having mine and not someone else's? It is, says Aquinas, the relationship in which that thought stands not only to other thoughts of mine, but also and primarily to my body, the body whose interactions with the world have provided the perceptions from which my thought begins. My identity is the identity of an animal body. My mind has its identity as the mind of this particular body. So my identity as a thinker is secondary to and derivative from my identity as a body. It follows that the mind cannot understand itself except as the mind of this particular body. But this at once sharply distinguishes Aquinas's position from that of Plato or Plotinus.

An act of thought is an act of this particular soul only because this soul is the soul of this particular body. Even a soul separated from its body by the dissolution of that body at death still derives its identity from its relationship to that body, so the relationship between soul and body and between mind and body is not, as it is with Plato and Plotinus, contingent and accidental. Moreover without the body the soul as the soul of this body is incomplete. It lacks something necessary for its perfected functioning. So soul needs to be reunited with body and God provides what is needed by the resurrection of the body. In his commentary on St. Paul's first letter to the Corinthians, Aquinas wrote: "If we deny the resurrection of the body, it is not easy—indeed it becomes very difficult to defend the immortality of the soul. The union of the body and soul is certainly a natural one. So if soul is deprived of body, it will exist imperfectly . . ." and "even if soul achieves well-being in another life, that does not mean that I do . . ." for "soul is not the whole human being, only part of one: my soul is not me" (McDermott 1993, 192–23).

What then is it to be this particular kind of being, a unity of body and soul with powers of mind and powers of action? What is it to be at once a changing material body among other material bodies in space and time and a being capable of knowledge of God, who is unchanging and eternal? It is to understand oneself as goal directed, as one who moves by one's nature from one's point of material origin toward theoretical and practical final ends, the ends of knowing and of loving God. The vision of God fulfills and completes our enquiries as rational beings, those enquiries that express our desire to understand. According to philosophers, says Aquinas, the ultimate perfection that the soul can attain is "to have inscribed in it the whole order and causes of the universe. This they took to be the ultimate end of a human being, the end that on our view of it will be the vision of God, because, as Gregory puts it, 'What is there that they do not see who see him who sees everything?'" (*Questiones Disputatae de Veritate* 2.2). The love of God that is inseparable from that vision, since to know God is to love him, is already present in some lives in that charity that is the form of all the virtues and the virtues are just those qualities that we need in order to achieve our good. That these are the ends to which our human nature is directed is however something that we as rational agents have to learn. We do have the powers needed to learn how to understand and how to act, so that we may achieve those ends to which we are directed by our nature, but it is up to us whether or not we develop those powers in the right way. How then do we learn and how do we develop those powers?

We find ourselves in a material world, trying to understand the particulars that confront us and trying to achieve those goods without which we will be unable to sustain ourselves in that material world, let alone to flourish. The route to understanding lies through answering the questions that Aristotle's fourfold scheme of causality invites us to ask. The route to achieving our goods lies through identifying those common goods that we share with other human beings who are also trying to understand and trying to achieve their goods. And it turns out that we need theoretical understanding, not only for its own sake, but also for its practical relevance.

The universe of particulars that we confront presents itself to us as intelligible, as providing answers to our questions. So—and Aquinas is here carrying further a line of argument first developed by ibn Sīnā and ibn Rushd—we can move from identifying what kind of thing some particular is (Aristotle's formal cause) and whatever purpose or function it serves (Aristotle's final cause) to asking what it is made of (Aristotle's material cause) and what agency has bought it into being and made its characteristics what they are (Aristotle's efficient cause). But, as we noted earlier, when we have provided an initial explanation in these terms, we discover that it is incomplete. Even if we have correctly identified the agency or agencies the exercise of whose causal powers made this particular what it has been and is, we still need an explanation of how this particular agency was able to and did exert its causal power to this particular effect. But if we provide such an explanation by identifying further causes, we still have the question of how those further causes had the powers that *they* had and employed them as they did. So we seem to have embarked on the project of constructing an indefinitely long chain of causal explanations, each of them incomplete.

Aquinas, in expounding the third of what he takes to be five ways in which we may reason our way from premises concerning particulars to the conclusion that God exists, points out that the causal agencies that we cite in those explanations may be of two kinds. They may be—and most of them are—contingent beings, beings which could have been other than they are and could have operated other than as they do. That they are as they are and that they operate as they do depends upon some other causal agency acting on them. Or they may be beings that necessarily are as they are and operate as they do, but this in virtue of some other causal agency from which this necessity is derived. In both cases such beings depend for their existence and operations upon something else. Suppose then that our universe consists of an infinite chain of such dependent beings and their operations—and of nothing else. This infinite chain of dependent beings is itself explanation demanding, that is, it too has the characteristics of dependent beings. Therefore, for it to exist, there has to have been and to be something else, that on which it depended and depends for its existence. But, *ex hypothesi*, on this supposition our universe consists of an infinite chain of dependent beings and of nothing else. So we must conclude that our universe, if it consisted only of dependent beings, would not have existed. But it exists. From this it follows that there must exist something that is not a dependent being.

What would something be that was not a dependent being? It not only would exist necessarily, that is, it could not have not existed, but it would depend on nothing external to it for its existence and its characteristics. It would be entirely self-determining and there could be and would be no need of and no place for any explanation of how it came to be, for it could not have come to be, since everything that comes to be depends on something else for its existence. If the argument that we have sketched is sound then, given that there are dependent beings, there must be just such a necessary being. For otherwise nothing would have existed.

This, says Aquinas, everyone speaks of as God (*Summa Theologiae* Ia, 2.3). The argument, we should note, does not show that God, so understood, *created* the world of finite beings. So far as rational enquiry is concerned, it remains an open question, just as Aquinas contended, whether or not the world has existed eternally. What the argument does show, so Aquinas holds, is that, even if the universe had no beginning in time, it depends and has depended for its continuing existence at every moment on God. But is the argument sound? And how might atheists respond to it?

The atheists' quarrel with this argument, like their quarrel with ibn Sīnā and ibn Rushd, may first of all focus on the conceptions of intelligibility and of explanation that are presupposed by it and they will appeal against those conceptions to a range of modern conceptions of explanation advanced by philosophers of science: Kantian and Neo-Kantian or empiricist or material- ist or positivist. What those appeals have in common is a rejection of the possibility of finding application for the concepts of cause and effect beyond the world of nature as it is presented in sense experience. The natural uni- verse, the set of finite beings, is, so they claim, not something to which we can meaningfully attribute a cause. Indeed some have argued that we cannot speak meaningfully of the set of all finite beings. And so Aquinas, by arguing that God, not himself a finite being, is the sustaining cause of the continuing existence of all finite beings, both attempts to extend the application of the notions of cause and effect unjustifiably and to use the nature of a totality of finite beings illegitimately.

Yet perhaps the onus is now on the atheist to demonstrate that the argu- ments for these conclusions are sound. No arguments advanced in order to demonstrate this, whether Kantian or empiricist, materialist or positivist, have turned out to be incontestable. Indeed the representatives of each of these positions have advanced arguments some of whose premises are rejected by the representatives of the other three. Yet at this point it would be premature for Thomistic theists to conclude that they have therefore emerged from the debate with their central argument for the existence of God unscathed, for there is a set of questions about the conclusion of that argument that have not yet been asked.

When we assert that God exists, we do indeed need to give an account of what we mean by 'God,' but we also need to give an account of what we mean by 'exists.' We may assert or deny the existence of beings of very different kinds: of physical objects, such as pebbles, cabbages, and tigers; of immaterial objects, such as angels, of numbers and sets; and of God, who is so very different from all other beings that he is said not to be of a kind, not to be a member of a class. What account does Aquinas give of the relations between these different types of assertion of existence and of what it is that we mean when we assert—or deny—that God exists?

We mean or should mean something very different from what we mean when we say of any finite being that it exists. To say of such a being that it exists is to say that it is a being (*ens*) and that it participates in being (*esse*). Since this holds of every such being, we may speak of *ens commune* and of *esse commune*. But neither of these concepts has application to God. Of finite beings it is true that they are what they are because their essence—what they are—has been realized in existence, an act of existence that has the finite, that is, limited form that it has, just because their particular essence is the essence that it is. What it is to be a pebble or a cabbage or a tiger or an angel determines the character of the particular finitude of each. With God, however, it is quite otherwise, both in respect of our knowledge of him and in respect of his existence.

To understand pebbles, cabbages, tigers, and angels is to understand what they are, to grasp their essential properties. But God is beyond our understanding. We cannot have the kind of knowledge of him that we have of finite beings, and this at least in part is because we cannot apply to him the distinction between essence and existence. God's existence is not limited by his essence, as finite beings are, beings that possess some perfections in some particular modes, but lack other perfections in other particular modes. God by contrast is unlimited in his perfections and what he is, his essence is identical with his existence, not a limitation upon it. Hence the actuality of God's existence is quite different from the actuality of pebbles, cabbages, tigers, and angels. In ascribing actual existence to both we use expressions such as "exists" analogically, and we extend this analogy further in speaking of the existence of numbers and sets. So, as we noticed earlier in discussing Anselm's arguments, we say a good deal more and other in asserting of something that it exists, whether God or some material object or some number, than we would assert if we were speaking of existence as the existential quantifier speaks of it. (In this account I have followed closely the discussion of these issues by John Wippel in *The Metaphysical Thought of Thomas Aquinas* [2000], especially pp. 122–24 and 172–75, and Fran O'Rourke in chapter 6 of his *Pseudo-Dionysius and the Metaphysics of Aquinas* [2005].)

God then is being itself (*ipsum esse subsistens*), He Who Is. We should note that in thinking about God in this way Aquinas had transcended the limitations of Aristotelian modes of thought and recognized conceptual possibilities that were unknown and alien to the philosophers of the ancient world. It is here that Aquinas's theology is important. Without that theology he would not have been able to ask some of the key philosophical questions he addressed, such questions as that of what reason we have to assert that the God who reveals himself exists, how it is that human beings are directed by their nature toward an end beyond nature, and that, even although God is omnipotent, finite beings, including human beings, have independent powers of causal agency. In the course of addressing such questions Aquinas found it necessary also to investigate issues of meaning, of truth, and of rationality. In each case Aquinas begins from the philosophical resources that Aristotle and the Islamic and Jewish commentators on Aristotle had provided. But in each there comes a point at which he could only progress further by going beyond Aristotle. To be a Thomist therefore is always to be an Aristotelian, but also to go beyond Aristotle, just as Aquinas did.

Cited Works by Thomas Aquinas

Summa contra Gentiles
Summa Theologiae
Quaestiones Disputate de Anima
Quaestiones Disputatae de Veritate

References

McDermott, Timothy, trans. *Aquinas: Selected Philosophical Writings*. Oxford: Oxford University Press, 1993.

O'Rourke, Fran. *Pseudo-Dionysius and the Metaphysics of Aquinas*. Leiden: E. J. Brill, 1992; Notre Dame, IN: University of Notre Dame Press, 2005.

Wippel, John. *The Metaphysical Thought of Thomas Aquinas*. Washington, DC: Catholic University of America Press, 2000.

CHAPTER TEN

~

Aquinas: Philosophy and the Life of Practice

In Aquinas's account of the mind, human beings engage in two kinds of thinking, theoretical and practical. Theoretical enquiry aims at understanding and therefore at truth. A mind attains to the truth about some subject matter insofar as that mind is informed by and conforms to that subject matter, judging of it that it is as it is. And things are what they are independently of the mind's judgments about them. But truth is only one aspect of the final good that human beings seek.

We are by our nature directed to an end beyond nature, that of achieving not only truths about, but also the vision of God and with it a perfected love of God. In order to achieve this we must have those excellences of mind and character that will enable us to achieve that vision and that love. Aquinas's account of those excellences, that is, of the virtues, draws not only upon Aristotle, but also upon Plato and Augustine. In his identification of the four cardinal virtues, temperateness, courage, justice, and prudence, he follows Plato. In his account of the nature of particular virtues and of their various aspects and parts he is often indebted to Aristotle. In his discussion of the supernatural virtues, faith, hope, and charity, and of their relationships to the natural virtues, he characteristically follows Augustine. The moral virtues of temperateness, courage, and justice are acquired through habituation. We become temperate, courageous, and just by performing those actions that temperateness, courage, and justice require. What actions temperateness, courage, and justice require we initially learn from others. So characteristically and generally in order to be morally virtuous we need teachers—parents or other adults—who are themselves virtuous. We cannot have any of the moral virtues adequately unless we also learn to have prudence, the only virtue that is both a moral and an intellectual virtue. For without prudence we lack that capacity for right judgment, rightly directed feeling, and right action without which dispositions to act temperately, courageously, and justly will not issue in genuinely temperate, courageous, and just actions. So, as we acquire prudence, we may no longer seem to need teachers.

Yet we certainly need teachers at least up to this point: parents, other adults, and, to us more surprisingly, law. How then does Aquinas understand law and how can law be a teacher of the virtues? On Aquinas's account the precepts of law are precepts of reason directed toward the common good enacted and promulgated by someone with authority to do so (*Summa Theologiae* Ia–IIae, 90). The eternal law is that by which God rules the universe. That in his eternal law that has application to human beings we apprehend either by reason as the natural law or by faith as God's revealed law, revealed first as the Old Law on Sinai to Moses, and then as the New Law in the Sermon on the Mount by Jesus Christ. The law that human rulers of cities and kingdoms enact and enforce Aquinas calls human law. What are Aquinas's reasons for giving this kind of account of law?

The precepts of law are intended to govern human beings, animals with the powers of reason. We may try to govern a human being as a nonhuman animal is governed, by uttering imperatives, rewarding conformity, and penalizing disobedience. But if we are to govern any human being qua human being, it must be by appeal to his or her reasoning powers. Of any rule by which human beings are to guide their actions they and we may ask what reason there is for them to obey it. To say that a law is a precept of reason is to say that it is the kind of rule that there are good reasons to obey. It does not follow that a law may not be enforced by punishments or made acceptable by rewards. But insofar as laws are obeyed only because of punishments or rewards, they are not being acknowledged as laws, as precepts of reason.

There is good reason to obey a rule only when by so doing we achieve or move toward the achievement of some good. The goods that give point and purpose to laws are common goods, goods that we achieve not qua individuals, but qua members of some community or participants in some cooperative activity, the common goods of, for example, family life or of the life of a political community. Common goods are to be contrasted with individual goods. The common good of a family or a political community is not the sum of the individual goods of the members of that family or that community, qua individuals. They are goods that individuals can only achieve qua member of a family or qua member of a political community.

For any particular community only those who have the authority to do so can enact laws: "To order something to the common good is for the whole community or for someone acting on behalf of the whole community. Therefore to legislate is either for the whole community or for someone acting on behalf of the whole community" (*Summa Theologiae* 90.3). There are various forms of legitimate government, whereby one or more individuals are given authority to act on behalf of the community. So a king may have such authority entrusted to him or the members of some small group of rulers with the appropriate virtues, but the best form of government is a mixture of kingship, aristocracy, and democracy, in which a good king presides over a group of rulers, but election to office is open to all and is by all (*Summa Theologiae* 105.1).

Fourth and finally, laws enacted and enforced by such authorities must be promulgated. Human beings as rational agents cannot conform to a rule of which they are unaware. Hence, when a particular law has been enacted, it must be published in such a way that those to whom the law applies can become aware of it. God makes us aware of the precepts of the natural law as binding upon us by enabling us to grasp them as precepts of reason and so promulgating them.

The precepts of the natural law are divided into two classes. A set of primary precepts require us to respect and pursue certain goals and to avoid and refrain from the corresponding evils. They include such precepts as those that forbid the taking of innocent life, theft, and lying. The secondary precepts are those needed to apply the primary precepts to particular cases in particular social circumstances. It is, for example, a primary precept of the natural law that rulers should do whatever is necessary to provide for the security and defense of the territory for which they have responsibility. But the precepts that they will have to follow in order to provide for this will differ with time and place, depending upon the kind of threats their society faces, the resources available to them, and the level of weapons technology. So the secondary precepts of natural law vary from society to society and sometimes within societies, while the primary precepts are one and the same for everyone at all times.

By developing habits of obedience to the natural law, habits that are also expressed in the exercise of the virtues, we direct ourselves toward the achievement not only of the common goods of social life, but also of our individual good, that good by the achievement of which our lives are perfected and completed. Human beings often misconceive the nature of that good. In the opening sections of the first part of the second part of the *Summa Theologiae* (2.1–8; 3.6; 4.6–7) Aquinas catalogs twelve different conceptions of what the human good is, each of which would dictate a different way of life, and eleven of which he takes to be in error. Among these misdirected ways of life are those that would make the principal good to be the acquisition of money or the accumulation of power or the achievement of fame and glory or the pursuit of sensual pleasure or the perfecting of the human body. Those who in their everyday practice presuppose one of these mistaken views of the human good will also and consequently misunderstand the precepts of natural law.

That this is so and that therefore there are bound to be disagreements about what the precepts of the natural law are and how they are to be applied Aquinas was certainly aware. He recognized that there were cultures, such as that of the ancient Germans, whose moral code was in some respects at variance with natural law. But he did not know about and could not have known about the wide range of striking moral disagreements of which our modern knowledge of other cultures and their various histories has made us aware. If Aquinas had had to confront the facts of moral disagreement, what resources would he have been able to bring to bear on the difficulty that they may seem to pose for his account of natural law? The difficulty is this: whereas Aquinas claims that all human beings, qua rational agents, know what the unchanging precepts of the natural law are and that knowledge of those precepts cannot be erased from the human heart, large numbers of human beings reject those precepts. How on Aquinas's view is this to be explained?

Consider first what is involved in pursuing one's good as a rational agent. It is of crucial importance in deliberating as to how to act here and now that we deliberate in the company of other people, something that Aristotle had noted and that Aquinas emphasizes. For only thus will we escape from the one-sidedness of our own individual standpoint, only thus will the full range of relevant considerations be brought into play. But rational deliberation in the company of others is only possible, if both we and those others are committed to securing agreement only through the force of rational argument, only by, so far as possible, treating as good reasons for acting in this way rather than that what are in fact good reasons. So we must rule out from the beginning any attempt to arrive at agreement by use of coercive force or the threat of such force or by some mode of nonrational persuasion. The common mind at which we seek to arrive must not be the outcome of violence or of seduction, but of rational debate. Yet this outcome is possible only if the participants in such deliberation are committed and are seen by others to be committed to observing certain rules unconditionally and without exception. What rules would these be?

They would have to be rules prohibiting the taking of innocent life and the use of violence against the property and liberty of others and enjoining truthfulness and candor in deliberation. They would have to include rules prohibiting one from making commitments to others that one does not expect to fulfill and that bind one to keep whatever promises one might have made. Since they are to be rules without which genuinely rational deliberation would be impossible, they would have to be rules that would inform one's social relationships with anyone with whom one might at some time have to enter into shared deliberation, that is, with anyone whatsoever. But this set of precepts turns out to be identical with the precepts that Aquinas identifies as the precepts of natural law, so that as rational agents we are, just as Aquinas concluded, committed to conformity to the precepts of the natural law. But these are not the only commitments that we must make in order to engage in rational deliberation.

When we try to act in conformity with the precepts of natural law, we discover that in order to do so we need also to exercise the virtues. For it is only through the exercise of virtues that we know how to apply rules to particular cases. To be truthful it is not enough to refrain from telling lies. We also need to know which truths to utter to whom, when to speak and when to be silent, and the like. To observe those rules that require us not to be influenced unduly by our fears or by our appetites for pleasure we need to be courageous and temperate. So in those activities through which we learn what the law requires of us, we learn too our need of and how to exercise virtues. It is in this way that the law, whether natural law or positive law that gives expression to natural law, educates us and it is only insofar as we become virtuous that we are able to act as rational agents in deliberate agreement with other rational agents.

Moral disagreement, by contrast, especially radical disagreement, is always rooted in some failure to satisfy the conditions necessary for rational deliberation and therefore for rational agreement and rational agency. That is to say that its source is always in some response to the distracting solicitations of an undue and excessive love of money or power or pleasure or fame or the like that has undermined our practical reasoning, so that we fail to understand what the precepts of natural law require of us. It is these same motives that lead to recurrent violations of natural law, even by those who understand very well what the precepts of natural law require of them. We are all of us on various occasions so moved by such wayward desires that, blatantly or covertly, we allow our reasoning to be obscured and confused and our will to be directed toward some object of the relevant desire rather than to the good to the achievement of which it would be directed, if we were adequately rational. It is because this is so that over and above the cardinal virtues of prudence, temperateness, courage, and justice we also need the theological virtues of faith, hope, and charity.

It is in the end up to us whether or not we become prudent, temperate, courageous, and just. It is not at all up to us whether or not we receive the gifts of faith, hope, and charity, virtues that we owe entirely to divine grace, grace offered to us by God, virtues that are infused in us rather than acquired through habituation. Yet charity is, says Aquinas, the form of all virtues. Wherever there is genuine virtue, it is informed by charity and grace is at work. So that a purely secular understanding of the moral life is always inadequate and incomplete, both with regard to its end, the vision of God—the most that reason can show is that no finite object or state of affairs could be our final good—but also with regard to the kind of character that we need to have, if we are to become able to attain that end.

Who was Aquinas addressing in writing his moral philosophy and his moral theology? In the first instance of course his own students and the early readers of his published manuscripts. But it was argued compellingly by the great Thomistic scholar Leonard Boyle, OP, that Aquinas's larger purpose was to replace the older manuals that had guided pastors in the moral advice that they gave (1982). We should therefore understand him as addressing also, even if indirectly, all those plain persons who might in time be influenced by his students and his readers. So as a teacher in universities and in Dominican houses of study he contributed to the common life and the common goods of the larger communities of which he was a member, thus himself obeying the precepts of the natural law, and himself directing himself toward his natural and supernatural end, by the way in which he wrote about natural law and about human ends. The writing of the *Summa Theologiae* was an act of obedience to the precepts identified and explained in the *Summa*.

Cited Work by Thomas Aquinas

Summa Theologiae

Reference

Boyle, Leonard, OP. *The Setting of the Summa Theologiae of Saint Thomas*. Toronto: Pontifical Institute of Mediaeval Studies, 1982.

CHAPTER ELEVEN

~

Aquinas: God, philosopy, universities

Universities were to become, indeed by the thirteenth century already were, the socially designated caretakers of knowledge and understanding, not only institutions within which the different academic disciplines are pursued and taught, but also institutions that by their structure exhibit some view of how the different disciplines are related, of what it is in which the unity of knowledge and understanding consists. The history of universities since the thirteenth century has been at once a history of the development of the different disciplines and a history of transformations in beliefs about the relationships between the disciplines. Universities are therefore scenes of recurrent conflict, since both the development of particular disciplines and the transformations in how the relationships between the disciplines are conceived are marked by recurrent conflict.

In the University of Paris in Aquinas's time, one focus of contention is the place of philosophy—that is, of Aristotelian philosophy and natural science—in the arts curriculum. Over time the study of the older liberal arts is partially replaced by and partially integrated into a program of philosophical study in which Aristotle's logic, physics, ethics, and metaphysics all find a place and in which enquiry in each of these areas begins to take on a life of its own, formulating its own problems and posing solutions to them in a piecemeal way. Nonetheless in Paris and elsewhere—most notably Oxford—the arts curriculum continues to have a real unity, in part because of the shared Aristotelian vocabulary and concepts in terms of which problems are framed and in part because the arts curriculum is understood to be a prologue to theological studies, even if many of the students in the arts faculties never in fact proceeded to the study of theology, some of them moving to the study of law or medicine, many of them never going beyond the arts curriculum.

It would therefore not be a mistake to regard the thirteenth- and four-teenth-century university, at least at Paris and Oxford, as presupposing in its curriculum a conception of the unity of knowledge and understanding, of the relationships between the disciplines. Yet at once this claim requires qualification. For the indeterminacy of this conception becomes clear, if we compare the academic practices of Paris and Oxford with Aquinas's view of how teaching and learning should be organized. The student is, so Aquinas enjoins, to begin with the acquisition of the skills in grammar and logic provided by the teachers of those liberal arts. Logic includes all questions of method and is a prologue to the study of mathematics understood as an exercise of the imagination, its concepts and truths holding independently of experience, even although in formulating them we abstract from experience. From mathematics the student is to return to experience in the studies of the natural sciences. It is only when those logical, mathematical, and scientific studies have been completed that the student will be able to engage fruitfully in the enquiries of moral and political philosophy. For such enquiries require both a kind of experience of life that the younger student does not yet possess and the kind of maturity that enables one to be adequately reflective about one's passions. Only after this is the student in a position to engage with the enquiries of metaphysics and theology, enquiries that take us beyond the imagination and require peculiar strength of intellect (*Commentary on the Nicomachean Ethics* VI, lect.VII, 1209–11).

What is the point and purpose of this ordering? For most of the students at Paris, Oxford, or elsewhere the point and purpose of their studies was—as it has been with students ever since—to acquire whatever qualification was needed, if they were to proceed successfully to the next stage in their chosen future career. For many therefore the point of their studies was—and is—to put those studies behind them. But from Aquinas's view the point and pur-pose of a university education is to teach students that such a view of their studies is mistaken, that their studies are or should be designed to direct them toward the achievement of their final end as human beings, toward the achievement of a perfected understanding. And it was with this aim in view that Aquinas proposed this ordering of the different disciplinary enquiries.

What happens to a student when teaching and learning are well con-ducted and well ordered? The teacher initiates learning, but a good teacher follows the same order in teaching that students would follow in learning, if able to do so by themselves (*Questiones Disputatae de Veritate* ix.1). The aim is for students to develop into self-teachers, such that their exercise of their intellectual and moral powers enables them to become independent theoretical and practical reasoners. The ordering of the disciplines is designed not only with an eye to the relationships between the subject matter of the disciplines, but also with an eye to the ways in which the students' powers need to be developed.

The ends of education, that is to say, can, on Aquinas's view, be correctly developed only with reference to the final end of human beings and the ordering of the curriculum has to be an ordering to that final end. We are able to understand what the university should be, only if we understand what the universe is. But, while this thought was crucial for Aquinas's conception of the university, it was remarkably uninfluential in determining how universities in fact developed. It lived on in Dominican teaching and learning, but late medieval universities and their curricula were shaped by a variety of influences that left them inhospitable, or at least not particularly hospitable to Thomistic thought, until the great revival of interest in and study of Aquinas in Spanish universities in the sixteenth century.

Cited Work by Thomas Aquinas

Quaestiones Disputatae de Veritate

Reference

Aristotle. *Commentary on the Nicomachean Ethics.*

~

CHAPTER TWELVE

After Aquinas: Scotus and Ockham

Because Aquinas's thought, both his theology and his philosophy, has been of such central importance to Catholics since the late nineteenth century, we may be misled into thinking that it was similarly regarded in his own time. But this would be a mistake. Within his own Dominican order his influence was, even in his own lifetime, remarkable. But for most of those engaged in the intellectual debates of the thirteenth century and for their fourteenth-century successors, Aquinas's theses and arguments were treated as just one more contending set of positions, positions rejected by most. Indeed to many Augustinian theologians, especially to those in the Franciscan tradition, he seemed no more than one more Averroist.

In 1270 the bishop of Paris condemned a variety of propositions taught in the Faculty of Arts in the University of Paris and in 1277, after receiving advice from a commission of theologians, he renewed and enlarged this condemnation, identifying 219 propositions as heretical, some of them to be found in Aquinas's writings. At Oxford in the same year the archbishop of Canterbury issued a similar condemnation, including among the condemned propositions Aquinas's central thesis regarding the relationship of soul and body. In 1279 William de la Mare, a Franciscan friar, denounced 117 theses he ascribed to Aquinas in his *Correctorium fratris Thomae*, and in 1282 the Franciscans forbade the copying of Aquinas's *Summa Theologiae*, unless it was accompanied by the *Correctorium*.

Yet it was not just that Aquinas was from the outset a controversial figure. It was also remarkably easy to disregard his views. So when John Duns Scotus (ca. 1266–1308), the greatest of Franciscan thinkers and a very remarkable philosopher indeed, developed his own positions through the criticism of others, his chosen target was characteristically not Aquinas, but another theologian and philosopher who had taught at Paris, Henry of Ghent (ca. 1217–1293). Henry had been a member of the commission that had advised the bishop of Paris on the condemnations of 1277. His own theology and philosophy combined Augustinian and Aristotelian elements. Among the theses that Scotus attributed to Henry was the claim that no concepts have application both to God and to created finite beings: when we speak of God we mean one thing by our ascriptions, when we speak of created beings we mean quite another. Against Henry, thus understood, Scotus argued that, if this were true of all our concepts, our speech about God would be emptied of determinate meaning. We would not know how to make inferences from our statements about God. Scotus therefore concludes that, when we speak of God, saying of him that he exists, our concept must be the very same concepts that we use of created finite beings so that our terms have the same meaning in both cases. It is not clear that Henry actually held the position that Scotus attributed to him and certainly Aquinas did not hold that position. Yet some commentators have supposed that the arguments that Scotus directed against Henry constitute a refutation not only of Henry, but also of Aquinas. This too is a mistake.

On Aquinas's view our use of terms in speaking of God and of finite beings—including our ascriptions of existence—is neither equivocal nor univocal, but analogical, meaning by this that each term has a range of closely related senses, and that, while we use some terms about God in one sense and about finite created beings in another, those senses are closely related, although not always in the same way. Yet that Scotus and Aquinas disagree about ascriptions of existence is of course evident—and this is far from their only disagreement. Consider three others.

According to Aquinas, when a human being is in good order, her or his will is determined by her or his intellect and the conclusions arrived at by practical reasoning determine whether or not the will is determined to act rightly. For Scotus, it is an essential property of the will that it is not and cannot be so determined. The will, whether it moves to right action or not, is self-determining. Of any action that the will proposes to itself it has the power to perform it and the power to refrain from performing it. The will has by nature an inclination (*affectio commodi*) to perform actions that are advantageous to it (*bonum sibi*). But it also has by nature an inclination (*affectio justitiae*) to do what should rightly be done (*bonum in se*). It is in the power of the will to act either in accordance with or inconsistently with either of these natural inclinations. Whatever reason someone has for acting is itself determined by the will's exercise of this power of choice. Scotus, in this account of the autonomy of the will, moves radically away from Aristotle. In so doing he both throws light on a salient feature of any Aristotelian view, such as Aquinas's, and poses what was to become a continuing problem for philosophy.

For any Aristotelian it makes sense to ask of any action: "What reason did the agent have for so acting and was it a sufficiently good reason?" and the answer to this question raises the further question as to why this agent in this kind of situation acted for sufficiently good reasons or failed so to act. But on any plain reading of Scotus's view, it seems that this question cannot arise. That the agent acted as she or he did, for whatever reason she or he may have had, is a matter of an act of will that has and can have no further explanation, a contention at odds not only with Aquinas's Aristotelianism, but also with our everyday modes of explanation and understanding. Yet Scotus posed inescapable questions. The relationships between intellect and will are complex, and Scotus shows us that Aquinas's account of them, even if correct, is incomplete and needs further development and perhaps revision.

A second area of disagreement between Scotus and Aquinas concerns the relationship of soul and body. Here Scotus agrees with Henry in taking the body to have its own form (*forma corporeitatis*), distinct from the form that is the soul. Human beings, on his view, do not have the kind of unity that Aristotle and Aquinas had ascribed to them—Scotus has his own account of that unity—and so philosophical problems are set concerning how soul and body are related and how interaction between them is possible. Yet, if soul and body are only incidentally related, as seems to follow from Scotus's account, then it seems to be much easier than it is for Aquinas to make sense of the soul's enjoying a nonbodily existence after death. For Aquinas, human souls without bodies are incomplete; not so, for Scotus.

Third, Scotus disagrees with Aquinas about individuation, about what it is to be this or that particular individual. Aquinas's account is in terms of matter and form. Every particular is, as Aristotle put it, a "this-such." The form of a particular makes it the kind of thing that it is, the "such" of the "this-such." The matter of a particular, what Aquinas calls its designated matter, matter with determinate dimensions, is what makes it a particular, something that can be referred to by the "this" of the "this-such." With human beings it is *this* soul that, being the form of its body, makes of *this* body an individual. Scotus by contrast took it that no form could confer or constitute the particularity or the identity of an individual. Individuals are the kind of things they are, have the nature they do, in virtue of some form. But something else is needed for their individuality, something that belongs to *this* individual and to no other. That something Scotus called "thisness" (*haecceitas*). But the introduction of the name "haecceitas" takes us no closer to a solution to the problem. Scotus did not solve the problem of individuality any more than Aquinas did.

Followers of Aquinas have good reason to be grateful to Scotus. By identifying problems of which Aquinas's treatment is either incomplete or incorrect, Scotus posed important questions about what resources Aquinas or, after him, the Thomistic tradition can bring to bear in addressing those particular problems. But, when we move from Aquinas's and Scotus's treatment of particular problems to their more general standpoint, larger issues arise. The differences between them on the relationship of body and soul are aspects of an even deeper rooted disagreement about the powers of natural reason and the division of labor between philosophers and theologians.

For Scotus, so far as the enquiries of natural reason are concerned, we know nothing of any life but this present mortal condition. It is by revelation alone that we know of a world to come. Scotus agreed with the Averroists that an essentially embodied mind would have to regard itself as mortal. But he rejects not only the Averroist—and also the Thomist—conceptions both of the body-soul and of the body-mind relationship, but also the Averroist claim that philosophers are competent to speak on those matters. It is only the theologian, drawing upon the resources of revelation, who is able to speak of what lies beyond death and of what it is about human beings that makes them other than mortal. For Scotus human beings, apart from revelation, have no reason to understand themselves as directed to an end beyond this present world. Where Aquinas argues that every form of happiness that can be achieved by human beings in this present world has to be understood as imperfect and incomplete, Scotus argues that this is so only from the standpoint of an intelligence whose point of view is that of a disembodied soul. By contrast it is, on Aquinas's view, as an essentially embodied soul that I understand myself as directed to an end other than, and greater than, the finite ends of this life.

Scotus's teaching secured him a large following in the later middle ages especially—and not only in the Franciscan order—and an even more numerous following in the seventeenth and eighteenth centuries. Some of his views and arguments have been influential in later secular philosophy, most notably perhaps his thesis that being is and must be ascribed univocally, a thesis powerfully reinterpreted by Gilles Deleuze in our own time. Scotus's later Franciscan followers presented his views and arguments as the articulation of a system, giving it the name 'Scotism,' so that Scotism and Thomism were presented as two rival scholastic systems. Yet this is misleading. For Scotus is philosophically—not theologically—a significantly less systematic thinker than Aquinas, someone who tends to address problems piecemeal, drawing on his predecessors in a creatively ad hoc manner.

In this respect he is followed by another philosophically remarkable Franciscan, William Ockham (1283–1347). Ockham's work shows Scotus's influence in other ways. Ockham agrees with Scotus and disagrees with Aquinas in holding that the soul is not the form of the body, that embodied human beings do not have the kind of unity that Aquinas ascribed to them. Ockham agreed with Scotus and disagreed with Aquinas in holding that the will is self-determining and that, insofar as we act for good or for bad reasons, it is because some act of the will is exercised in our choice of reasons. But in his account of concepts and language Ockham is very different from Scotus.

About universals Scotus had developed a view of his own. What the mind grasps as universal is in the particular that the mind perceives and aspires to understand, as a common nature that that particular shares with other particulars of the same kind, as Socrates and Plato both have the common nature of humanity. Universals qua universals have no existence outside the mind, but through them we understand the reality of common natures. This type of realism about common natures, as developed by Scotus, was, according to C. S. Peirce, an indispensable presupposition of all later theorizing in the natural sciences. Ockham by contrast rejected this or any other version of realism concerning universals. Anything that exists outside the mind is a particular. Universals are no more than names of sets of particulars that are in this or that respect similar to each other. Yet Ockham also held that such names, insofar as they capture genuine similarities, are not arbitrary, so even Ockham is not as radical a nominalist as he might have been. Yet, if Peirce's claim about Scotus's realism is to be taken seriously, there is a problem as to whether the language of scientific theorizing can be made intelligible in Ockham's terms.

Both Scotus and Ockham formulated questions and posed problems that uncover difficulties of which even the most distinguished of their philosophical predecessors had not been adequately aware. By so doing they defined a partial agenda for future philosophical enquiry. And, because they were Catholic philosophers, addressing issues concerning God and human nature that are inescapable for any Catholic thinker, their work has to be integral to any adequate conception of the Catholic philosophical tradition.

Both of them were, like Aquinas, university teachers, Scotus at Oxford and Paris, Ockham at Oxford until he was censured for heretical views. But the university curriculum was no longer quite what it had been in Aquinas's time. Then the debates within universities had been in key part about how much of the teaching of philosophy, and especially of Aristotle's texts, should be restricted to the teachers of the liberal arts and how much should be assigned to the teachers of the theology faculty. But in the fourteenth and fifteenth centuries, philosophy as a discipline had found its own place in the curriculum with the enlarged study of logic still within the preliminary liberal arts framework, followed by the study of the three divisions of philosophy, natural philosophy, ethics, and metaphysics.

How philosophical enquiry developed in the later middle ages after Scotus and Ockham varied from university to university. Logic flourished in a number of places and so, at universities as different as Oxford and Padua, did natural philosophy. But philosophical originality was exhibited primarily in the piecemeal treatment of a wide range of problems, most of which had their roots in attempts to work out the implications of belief in God's unlimited power. The kinds of tensions and conflicts that philosophical enquiry had generated in universities in the thirteenth century were, in the fourteenth and fifteenth centuries, a thing of the past. Universities were no longer the scene of conflicts important to the whole culture. It was in key part from outside universities and indeed initially from outside philosophy that the new conflicts and the new impulses to philosophical enquiry were to come.

THE THRESHOLD
OF MODERN PHILOSOPHY

~

CHAPTER THIRTEEN

From Scholasticism to Skepticism

Disagreement and conflict, social, political, intellectual, and moral, were central to the life of Europe in the High Middle Ages. But in the period of transition from the late medieval period to early modernity, the conflicts and disagreements were on a larger scale and of different kinds. So in the various prologues to the Reformation, and during and after the Reformation, theological and religious disagreements multiplied and intensified. With the large interpretative recovery of ancient culture in the Renaissance, rival and alternative literary and philosophical stances emerged. The transition from the impetus theories of late medieval physicists and the complexities of Ptolemaic astronomy to the cosmology of Copernicus and the physics of Galileo generated a quite new set of divisive issues.

Yet in the same period there were also strong pressures aimed at producing agreement and eliminating conflict. The rulers of emerging modern states were anxious to secure uniformity of belief among their subjects in order to safeguard themselves and their regimes from discord and possible rebellion. Theologians on occasion attempted to resolve their disagreements and to design schemes for church reunion. Debates on controversial issues, whether theological, philosophical, or scientific, were not always polemical. But the outcome of these attempts at reconciliation tended to be either enforced conformity or continuing and deepening disagreement. Where there was enforced conformity there was intellectual sterility and, since almost all universities were places of enforced conformity, universities ceased, with some notable but occasional exceptions, to be the places where intellectually fruitful and exciting enquiry and debate took place, although they still, for most participants in such enquiry and debate, provided the initial education that enabled them to engage in the controversies of their age.

Such enquiry and debate engaged thinkers and groups of thinkers in widely different parts of Europe. The invention of the printing press enabled thinkers to communicate with a much larger educated public, some of them in hitherto distant places. Intellectuals traveled more widely than ever before, so that what was thought and said in Poland or Scotland speedily became known in Italy and the Netherlands. Copernicus, who had been a student first at Kraków and then at Padua, served the king of Poland, whose subject he was. But his book, in which the first compelling arguments for the heliocentric system were set out, was published as a result of the efforts of a mathematician from Wittenberg, and the most important responses to it were in Denmark, Bohemia, and Tuscany.

What no educated person could remain unaware of was the continuing depth of disagreement over a wide range of topics and the apparently intractable character of the most important disagreements. But responses to this situation were of different kinds. At one extreme there were those who continued to work within whatever intellectual tradition it was in which they had been educated, developing its theses and arguments further, and entering into controversy on its behalf. At the other extreme were those who became skeptical about the power of rational argument to overcome disagreement and who as a result defended some version of philosophical skepticism. Catholic thinkers were found at both of these extremes.

Francisco de Vitoria (ca. 1485–1546) was a Dominican priest and a remarkable thinker in and upholder of the Thomistic tradition. When Vitoria was a student in Paris his teacher in theology had been Peter Crockaert who, instead of commenting on the *Sentences* of Peter Lombard, the text that for centuries had been the staple of Catholic theological education, lectured instead on Thomas Aquinas's *Summa Theologiae*. When, in 1526, Vitoria was appointed to the senior chair in theology at the University of Salamanca, he followed his teacher's example.

His originality was a matter of how he brought Aquinas's teaching to bear on disputed questions of his own time, especially in the areas of law and politics. Has the pope authority over temporal rulers so that he can give or take away their authority over this or that political society? Has the Holy Roman Emperor such authority? What laws govern the relationship between different political societies? Under what conditions is a ruler justified in going to war? Every one of these questions had implications not merely for political theory, but also for the practical reasoning and decision making of those with power.

Vitoria's premises are drawn from Aquinas. He follows Aquinas in distinguishing eternal law, divine law, the natural law, and civil law of particular political societies. Political societies exist for the sake of that kind of ordered life that is indispensable to human flourishing. Such an ordered life is possible only when there is the rule of civil law framed in accordance with natural law. So each people must confer authority on a ruler or rulers whose task is to enact and enforce such law. No one has legitimate authority over a people except a ruler or rulers so authorized and their authority is limited by the constraints imposed by natural law. Hence it follows that neither pope nor emperor can have the kind of temporal authority over other rulers that some had claimed for them.

What then of the relations between political societies? Here Vitoria developed the notion of an *ius gentium*, originally found in Roman law, a set of standards prescribed—like the rest of natural law—by natural reason, standards that forbid the use of violence against other political societies, unless one's own political society has been unjustly attacked or Christians are being persecuted or the innocent are being oppressed by a tyrant, someone who lacks legitimate authority as a ruler, because his actions are dictated not by natural law, but by his own will and desires.

Here, too, Vitoria's conclusions committed him to a particular standpoint in contemporary controversy. In 1492 Cristoforo Colombo, in search of a route to Asia, had undertaken a voyage financed by the rulers of Spain that led him to the Americas. In 1493, in response to a petition by the rulers of Spain and Portugal, Pope Alexander VI ruled that all land discovered in the Americas that lay to the west of a line one hundred leagues west of the Azores was to fall under the authority of the Spanish monarchs, while all land lying to the east of that line was assigned to the rule of the Portuguese monarchs, provided that these lands were inhabited by non-Christians. In 1520–1522 Mexico and in 1531–1532 Peru were conquered by Spaniards with great ruthlessness and brutality. Responding to the latter conquest and its aftermath, Vitoria wrote to his Dominican superior "that no business shocks me or embarrasses me more than the corrupt profits and affairs of the Indies" (Lawrance 1991, 331).

Vitoria's understanding of the requirements of the *ius gentium* led him to argue that the imposition of Spanish rule on the American Indians was illegitimate. All its purported justifications failed. The pope lacked the authority to confer rule over the American Indians on the kings of Spain. The fact that the Indians were not Christians is irrelevant. What determines political authority is natural law and natural law binds Christians and non-Christians equally. The Indians had not aggressed against the Spaniards, but the Spaniards against the Indians. If it were argued, as it was, that the Indians lacked the capacities of rational agents to rule themselves, the evidence afforded by their actions and their social institutions showed otherwise.

Vitoria had provided the philosophical resources needed for the campaign against the appalling injustices done to the Indians that was waged by his fellow Dominican, Bartolomé de Las Casas (1474–1566), author of *Historia de las Indias*, and bishop of Chiapas in southern Mexico. Las Casas' particular concerns were with the Spanish laws sanctioning the system of forced labor inflicted on the Indians, but he also put in question the legitimacy of Spanish claims to have political authority over them. In a key series of debates at Valladolid in 1550–1551 his principal opponent was Juan Ginés de Sepúlveda. Sepúlveda had studied in Italy as well as Spain and was the author of polemics against both Erasmus and Luther. He had translated two of Aristotle's works into Latin and his defense of Spanish dominion and Spanish practices in the Americas was Aristotelian. Sepúlveda followed Aristotle in arguing that there is a class of human beings who are "natural slaves." Their lack of natural capacities is such that they can only be directed toward good ends by rational agents who impose their authority upon them. Sepúlveda identified the American Indians as just such natural slaves and the Spaniards who had conquered the Americas as just such rational agents. Las Casas did not deny outright that there might be such natural slaves. But his firsthand experience of Indian life gave him the strongest grounds for rejecting the claim that the Indians fell into this category.

It was not only among the Dominicans that theses and arguments of the great medieval Catholic philosophers were developed further. Franciscan scholars had elaborated aspects of Scotus's teaching into a system, and in 1633 at Toledo a general chapter of the Franciscan order officially endorsed Scotism in both philosophy and theology. Scotus's commentary *Opus Oxoniense*, on the *Sentences* of Peter Lombard, became a prescribed text in universities in which Franciscans occupied chairs of theology. Scotism was presented as a rival of and superior to Thomism. But neither the Dominican Thomists nor the Franciscan Scotists of the sixteenth and seventeenth centuries were as influential as their Jesuit contemporary, Francisco Suárez (1548–1617).

Suárez drew not only on Aristotle and Aquinas, but also on Scotus, Ockham, and other medieval writers. He did so in order to construct his own distinctive philosophical standpoint. His *Disputationes Metaphysicae* was the first systematic account of metaphysics in European thought that was not a commentary on Aristotle's *Metaphysics*. On each issue he raised he summarized the relevant theses and arguments of his scholastic predecessors and then arrived at his own conclusions by subjecting theirs to criticism. So for many seventeen- and eighteenth-century thinkers Suárez became *the* representative figure of scholastic thought, the only one with whom they had to reckon in their own philosophical enquiries. Yet Suárez's synthesis also put him at odds with the heirs of all those philosophers to whom he was indebted, but of whom he was critical. So Suárez, being neither Thomist nor Scotist nor follower of Ockham, was at odds with Thomists, Scotists, and followers of Ockham.

Suárez affirmed that nothing existed except individuals. He agreed with Aquinas and disagreed with Scotus that being is predicated of individuals analogically. He disagreed with Aquinas in holding that we have a prereflective knowledge of individuals, one that is unmediated by universals. He disagreed with Vitoria in holding that the *ius gentium* is part of or derivable from natural law. And there are other significant items to be added to this catalog of disagreements among the rival heirs of medieval Catholic philosophy. What it is important to note is that these disagreements, just as much as the larger disagreements between those heirs and the several new schools of philosophy that arose during the Renaissance, were not resolved, that the protagonists of each standpoint remained convinced that they had sufficient reason to reject the conclusions of their opponents. Such unresolved and apparently irresolvable disagreements posed a radical question about the powers of human reason. It is unsurprising that the nature and limits of those powers became an urgent topic for philosophical debate and that skepticism, both in the forms in which it had flourished in the ancient world and in new forms, was able to present itself as a compelling philosophy.

Two quite different and incompatible types of skepticism have been ascribed to the first notable ancient Greek skeptic, Pyrrho of Elis (ca. 365–275 B.C.). The more radical is that which enjoins us to beware of the deliverances of sense-experience and memory, which may always mislead us, so that we can be certain of nothing and ought to doubt everything. Yet, although Diogenes Laertius ascribed this radical view to Pyrrho and mocked him for adopting it, it seems very unlikely that he did in fact hold it. He was more probably a moderate sceptic, arguing that those issues on which philosophers have disagreed are undecidable, that we cannot arrive at a true account of how things are, but that we should content ourselves with taking them as they seem to be, so avoiding fruitless enquiry and needless dispute. As between opposing opinions we must suspend both belief and disbelief.

It is this latter type of moderate skepticism that was revived in sixteenth-century France by Michel de Montaigne (1533–1592). Montaigne had experienced the devastation caused by so-called wars of religion, in which religious disagreements had been put to the service of secular political ambition and greedy self-interest. His hope was to neutralize religious polemic by making religious partisans less certain of the truth of their own opinions, so that opinion should no longer play a part in generating hatred and destruction. In his library he had put up the inscription: "Men are tormented by their opinions of things, not by things themselves." Montaigne's principal intention in deploying skeptical arguments, drawn from his reading of Sextus Empiricus, was to undermine some of the rival contentions of both Catholics and Protestants in their polemics against each other. So in his long essay on the Catholic theologian Raymond Sebond, Montaigne defended Sebond by arguing against his critics' arguments. Sebond held that natural reason, had it been uncorrupted by sin, would have been able to arrive at conclusions supportive of the Catholic faith, but that natural reason as it is, corrupted by sin, lacks this ability. Montaigne agreed with Sebond on this weakness of reason, although not on theological grounds. His follower, the lawyer and priest, Pierre Charron, carried Montaigne's philosophical project one stage further.

Charron was not the first Catholic sceptic. Gentian Hervet, the translator of Sextus Empiricus into Latin, and Francisco Sanches, a professor of medicine at Toulouse and Montaigne's cousin, had both anticipated him in arguing that skepticism undermines all arguments against the Catholic faith and so provides it with indirect support. Charron argued further that the only matters on which we can have certainty are those about which God has revealed truths and that only faith in the authoritative interpretation of that revelation by the Catholic church provides us with a certainly trustworthy account of those truths. What then are the types of argument on which Montaigne and these Catholic followers of his rely? They begin from the inescapable fact that philosophers and theologians have over long periods of time failed to resolve their disagreements and infer that there are no *conclusive* arguments on any of these disputed questions. They proceed beyond this to what Montaigne took to be the practice of the ancient Pyrrhonians, namely that of opposing to any assertion or argument whatsoever a counterassertion or counterargument, not in order to produce conviction, but in order to show that there are never adequate grounds for full assent.

If someone should try to generalize from this and to assert that one can indeed know nothing, they will quarrel with this, too. "If you conclude that you definitely know nothing, they will maintain that you do know something. Yes, and if you present your doubts as axiomatic, they will challenge you on that too, arguing that you are not in doubt, or that you cannot decide for certain and prove that you are in doubt. This is doubt taken to its limits. It shakes its own foundations . . . " (Montaigne 1987, 70).

Montaigne's *An Apology for Raymond Sebond* is in part an exercise in irony, an essay purporting to defend a theologian, while undermining not perhaps any theology, but any dogmatic theology. It is clear that Montaigne's skepticism does indeed preclude the kind of assent to doctrine that is required by the Catholic faith—and also by its Protestant opponents. But, if Montaigne's arguments are at odds with the Catholic faith, then the use of skeptical arguments by Hervet, Sanches, and Charron is equally, if unintentionally, subversive. If the Catholic faith is to be upheld as consistent with what reason requires, then there has to be some adequate philosophical reply to skepticism. It is not only theology that has this interest in showing skepticism to be unwarranted. In the disputes between the protagonists of Copernican astronomy and Galilean physics on the one hand and the defenders of the Neoaristotelian physics of the impetus theorists on the other, both parties recognized that what was at stake was the *truth* about nature. Suspension of belief and disbelief would not have been an acceptable outcome and would have done great harm to the development of the natural sciences. So it seemed that scientists and philosophers of science needed a refutation of skepticism as badly as theologians did. Enter Descartes.

References

Lawrance, Jeremy, trans. *Political Writings: Francisco de Vitoria.* Ed. Anthony Pagden and Jeremy Lawrance. New York: Cambridge University Press, 1991.

Montaigne, Michel de. *An Apology for Raymond Sebond.* Trans. M. A. Screech. London: Penguin Books, 1987.

CHAPTER FOURTEEN

~

Descartes, Pascal, and Arnauld

Montaigne, by his skepticism, distanced himself from the Catholic faith, moved by a wish to rid himself and others of the unhappy dogmatism of the contending parties in the sixteenth-century wars of religion. René Descartes, born at LaHaye in Touraine shortly after those wars had come to an end, was throughout his life a believing Catholic. He was educated at the Jesuit school at La Flèche, among the best schools in Europe at that time. His Jesuit teachers introduced him to philosophy, to mathematics—at which Descartes was to excel—to physics, and then to theology and in each case laid the foundations for his future intellectual development.

About philosophy what impressed him—like Montaigne, like Charron—was the inability of philosophers to agree. Hence was to spring his conviction that, if any genuine progress is to be made in philosophical enquiry, it must be made on the basis of truths that cannot but secure the agreement of any rational enquirer. The physics that he was taught, and which he came to reject very early on, was the Neo-Aristotelian physics of the Scholastic philosophers and in rejecting it he rejected all the rival schools of Scholastic philosophy. The theology of his Jesuit instructors was, in some broad sense, Augustinian, and Descartes's thought is informed throughout by Augustinian presuppositions, most notably in the way he follows Augustine's injunction to seek truth by moving away from sense experience in order to discover it within the mind (on Descartes's relationship to Augustine see Stephen Menn 1998).

After Descartes left La Flèche in 1614 his life was very much what we would expect of the son of a provincial landowner. He studied law at Poitiers and became a soldier. But his intellectual interests, especially in mathematics, still engrossed him and were developed through his own private reading and thinking and through extended conversations and correspondence with others. Although Descartes's intellectual achievements were exceptional, his reliance on and contributions to letters and conversations with colleagues and friends, who made each other aware of the latest developments in philosophy, mathematics, physics, and literature, who shared their work with each other and invited each other's criticism, was typical of his age. Universities were for the most part strongholds only of theology and of Scholastic philosophy and had become to varying degrees intellectually irrelevant.

For Descartes there was a sharp contrast between the contemporary progress being made in mathematics, in astronomy, and in physics, developments to which he himself from a relatively early age made striking contributions, and the lack of progress in philosophy, whatever the standpoint of the philosopher. It was this situation that he aspired to remedy by providing a new starting point for philosophical enquiry, one immune to skeptical doubt, one that could provide a set of foundations for the mathematical and physical sciences. But, if he was to make out a sufficiently compelling case against skepticism, he had first to provide the strongest possible case for it. So his philosophical project became that of constructing a framework within which skepticism could be both stated and refuted. His first great insight into how he might carry out his project came in 1619, while he was still a soldier in Germany, on a winter's day that he spent in a room behind the stove, making what he later called a "wonderful discovery." But it was to be quite a number of years before he provided a philosophical account of his first insights and the impulse to provide that account was reinforced by the influence of Cardinal Pierre de Bérulle, an Oratorian, and a major figure in the revival of Catholic piety in seventeenth-century France.

In 1628 Descartes was present at a gathering at which a physician named Chandoux had presented the principles of his own new philosophy, claiming for those principles "*vraisemblance*," plausibility, the appearance of truth. It was Descartes who demonstrated at that gathering the difference between plausibility and truth and the need to show that one's formulated principles were true and not merely plausible, since the plausibility of a principle is compatible with its falsity. Bérulle was enormously impressed and told him that, because God had given him great intellectual gifts, he, Descartes, would be responsible to God for his use or misuse of them. In a letter that Descartes wrote two years later to his friend, Marin Mersenne, priest and savant, Descartes explained the path that he had thenceforward taken, using the reason that God had given him to know God and to know himself (quoted in Menn 1998, 49–50).

Descartes begins within himself, with his awareness of what is directly presented to his mind, of the stock of ideas that he encounters when he inspects the contents of his mind. But then skeptical questions arise. Are things outside his mind such as these ideas represent them to be? Those things include not only the various inanimate objects, plants, and animals of which he has hitherto taken himself to have sense experience, on the basis of which he has formed his beliefs about them, but also his own body. So he asks: "Is it possible that in believing what I do about all of these I am deceived?" He takes himself to have strong reasons for answering, "Yes." We are all of us an occasion mistaken as to what we take ourselves to have perceived. We are sometimes deceived by hallucinations. When dreaming, we suppose ourselves to be awake and mistakenly take ourselves to be perceiving. We are sometimes in error in our reasoning, without recognizing the fact. So on any particular occasion I may be deceived without knowing it. And it may therefore seem to be the case that on any particular occasion I cannot know that this is not one more occasion on which I am in error. Hence I must doubt the truth of all my judgments.

Descartes allows that in everyday life we and he would all of us take such doubt to be unreasonable. But, if we are to find secure foundations for our beliefs, including our scientific beliefs, then we must find an answer to the strongest case that can be made for taking such doubts seriously. So Descartes at the end of the first of his *Meditations on the First Philosophy* imagines that there is an evil demon, as powerful as he is cunning, who is systematically deceiving him by contriving illusions of which he is the victim. Is there anything at all about which he could not be deceived by such a demon? Is there any judgment of whose truth he can certainly be assured?

Descartes replies that there is indeed such a truth and here he follows Augustine. Augustine had responded to the ancient skeptics who had asked "What if you are deceived?" by asserting that "if I am deceived, I am" (see chapter 5). So Descartes's reply to his own skeptical doubts is to assert: "I think, therefore I am" (*Cogito ergo sum; Je pense donc je suis*). For, if I doubt, the one thing that I cannot doubt is that I am doubting. And, since to doubt is to think, if I doubt, I am thinking. And, since I cannot think, unless I exist, if I think, I am. But what then is it that I know to exist? All that Descartes knows of himself so far is that he is a thinking thing. He is and knows himself to be a mind, but he does not as yet know whether or not anything exists other than his mind, including his body.

The properties of what, when he is not engaged in doubting, he takes to be his own body and other bodies are quite other than the properties of a mind. Bodies are extended, three dimensional, heavy or light, occupying space. Our knowledge of them, if it is indeed knowledge, comes from our sense experience. But Descartes so far has found reasons only to distrust his sense experience. His next problem then is to find grounds for trusting the deliverances of sense experience. The first step toward identifying these grounds is to reinspect the contents of his mind, finding among his ideas that of an infinite and perfect being, God.

Descartes had identified clarity and distinctness as marks of the truth of the ideas expressed by the Cogito. The very same clarity and distinctness, so he claims, belongs to the idea of God, an idea such that no one whose grasp of its clarity and of what makes it distinct from every other idea can fail to recognize it as the idea of something that must exist outside the mind. Descartes advances two different kinds of argument. First, he argues that just as to grasp the idea of a triangle is to understand that necessarily its three angles add up to 180 degrees, so also to grasp the idea of God is to understand that God must necessarily exist. Second, he argues that the idea of an infinite and perfect being has properties such that its presence in the mind could only have been caused by just such a being, so that the idea of God itself directs us to the reality of God.

Were these arguments of Descartes sound, his further contentions might have been compelling. For such a perfect being, so Descartes contends, could not and would not deceive us by permitting us to have deceptive sense experience. We ourselves may make incautious judgments about what is presented to us in sense experience and these judgments may as a result be in error. But God ensures that sense experience itself is trustworthy and therefore that what we have taken to be knowledge of bodies is indeed knowledge. So anyone who follows Descartes's procedure, beginning from within the mind and arguing her or his way through the Cogito, the arguments for the existence of God, and the argument for the existence of bodies will, so Descartes claims, have defeated the sceptic. Our confidence in our everyday beliefs will have been justified and foundations will have been laid for the enquiries of the physicists. But is Descartes right?

Everything turns on the arguments for the existence of God and those arguments fail. The first is simply fallacious. What we understand, once we have grasped the idea of a triangle, is that, if anything is a triangle, then necessarily its three angles add up to 180 degrees. But we are not entitled to conclude that there are any triangles. What in parallel fashion we understand, when we have grasped the idea of God, is that, if God exists, then he exists necessarily. But we are not entitled to conclude that God exists. As for Descartes's further arguments, it is too unclear what Descartes means for us to arrive at any unqualified verdict. If those arguments were to be compelling, much more would have had to be said. Neither Descartes nor any subsequent Cartesian has said it. So that Descartes's chain of arguments breaks down after he has by means of the Cogito established a justification for his belief in his own existence as a thinking being, but before he has established a justification for his belief in God. Yet without sufficient grounds for belief in God Descartes takes himself to lack sufficient grounds for belief in anything at all outside his mind, including his own body. The victory over the skeptics accomplished by the Cogito is too limited a victory, and Descartes has not discovered a foundation for the natural sciences that is immune to skeptical doubt. Should this matter to us as well as to Descartes?

The answer is "No" and this for two reasons. The first is that skepticism does not require an answer. The skeptic's claim is that our beliefs and judgments are open to doubt, because it is always possible that we may be mistaken in believing as we do and in judging as we do, because there is always the possibility of error. But to point out—quite correctly—that it is possible that we are in error gives us no reason whatsoever to believe that we are in fact in error. And, until we are given such a reason, we have no reason whatsoever to doubt what we otherwise have good reason to believe and to judge. The skeptic's claim that we can only truly say, "I know that such and such" or "I am certain that such and such" or be entitled to assert that such and such, if there is *no* possibility at all of our being in error about how things are, is a claim that the sceptic has given us no good reason to accept. It follows that the natural sciences do not need the kind of foundation that Descartes aspired to provide for them.

That this is so becomes even clearer when we consider what kind of foundation a natural science does need and can have. Every science aims at the achievement of a perfected understanding of its particular subject matter. To achieve such a perfected understanding is to be able to make some set of phenomena—tides, thunderstorms, glaciers, the firing of neurons in the brain, the production of chemical reactions in the bloodstream, falling rates of economic growth, or rising rates of violent crime—intelligible and explicable as the outcome of whatever are the fundamental determinants of those phenomena. The concepts and the generalizations through which we identify those fundamental determinants and the complexities of their relationships to the particular phenomena are what provide each particular science with its foundations.

However, what we have learned from the history of science—something that neither Aristotle nor Descartes were in a position to learn—is that over time in the course of our scientific enquiries our conception of what it would be to achieve a perfected understanding of this or that set of phenomena changes. We find that we have good reason to reject or to revise, sometimes radically, our earlier accounts of what the foundations, the first principles, of this particular science are. But, until and unless we find that we have good reason to do so, we have no reason to put in question our present understanding of those foundations. The knowledge that we may later on need to reject or to revise—the knowledge, that is, of our own fallibility—of itself gives us no reason to reject or revise.

The skeptical challenge was therefore a phantom challenge. Happily it almost immediately ceased to influence philosophers at work within the Catholic tradition. Catholic skepticism was soon recognized as the aberration that it was and attempts to respond to the skeptical challenge were seen to be fruitless, although not perhaps for the reasons that I have given. The principal cause of the dismissal of skepticism in French seventeenth-century philosophy may have been the very different response to it by Blaise Pascal (1623–1662). Pascal, having surveyed the arguments of the skeptics and concluded that there was no way to answer them, asked, "What then is man to do in this state of affairs? Is he to doubt everything?" and replied: "No one can go that far, and I maintain that a perfectly genuine sceptic has never existed. Nature backs up helpless reason and stops it going so wildly astray" (Pensées 1966, 64). We are so constituted, that is, that the arguments of the sceptic, even if unanswerable, carry no conviction. One can pretend to be a sceptic, but no one actually lives and acts as if skepticism were justified.

This inability both to refute the arguments of the sceptic and to accept them is for Pascal one more symptom of the paradoxical character of the human condition. On the one hand we human beings can be satisfied only by a perfected grasp of truth and the achievement of a happiness that is without flaw. We are by our nature inescapably directed toward these goals. Yet on the other hand we recurrently have to recognize that it is just these goals that we are unable to achieve and that our inability to achieve them is deeply rooted in what we are. It is only because we have a capacity for and an ineliminable desire for happiness that we are as unhappy as we are. It is only because we have the powers of reason and the ability to exercise them that we are able to understand that we cannot achieve the truth to which we aspire.

We try desperately to conceal from ourselves what our condition is. "The only good thing for human beings therefore is to be diverted from thinking of what they are, either by some occupation which takes their mind off it, or by some novel and agreeable passion which keeps them busy, like gambling, hunting, some absorbing show, in short by what is called diversion" (*Pensées* 1966, 136). So the lives of worldly human beings are devoted to a series of projects designed to disguise from them their unhappy state. To understand that unhappy state more adequately and why they are condemned to it is something that lies beyond their powers, so long as they remain in their worldly condition. So long as they remain in that condition, they deny themselves the self-knowledge they would need to recognize the nature of their diversions. How then might they achieve this kind of understanding and this kind of self-knowledge?

Pascal's answer is that these are to be achieved only by a change of heart, by conversion to belief in God and trust in Christ's saving work. Pascal himself had been brought up a devout Catholic. When he was twenty-three, he and his family were introduced to the pastoral theology of the Abbé de Saint-Cyran, who had been spiritual director to the nuns of the convent at Port Royal before his imprisonment and subsequent death in 1643. Pascal as a result came to believe that a worldly life, a life devoted to a professional career, for example, was incompatible with a Christian life. His acute sense of the division between these two ways of life, the one an expression of the need for diversions and so of the divided and unhappy nature of human beings, the other an expression of contrition and of acceptance by God, was further sharpened by his experience on the night of November 23, 1654, which he recorded on a piece of parchment sown into his clothing that was found after his death.

In it he speaks of fire, certainty, and joy in the knowledge of God and of Jesus Christ. Two phrases from that record are relevant to his philosophy: "'God of Abraham, God of Isaac, God of Jacob,' not of philosophers and scholars" and "The world forgotten, and everything except God" (*Pensées* 1966, 309). The contrast between the God of Abraham, Isaac, and Jacob and the God of the philosophers expresses Pascal's conviction that any God about whom we judge that he exists because of some set of philosophical arguments would not be the God in whom we need to believe. The need to forget everything except God expresses his conviction that any kind of preoccupation with worldly concerns is a barrier between oneself and God. So it might appear that, on Pascal's view, there can be no intellectual justification for belief in God. But this is not so and in two different ways.

Pascal first of all believes that once we come to believe in God we become able to understand our human condition in a way that was previously denied to us and also to understand why, without belief in God, human beings are unintelligible to themselves and their nature an enigma. It is only as we come to know God that we come to know ourselves adequately, since what we are and have been is intelligible only in and through our relationship to God. So the justification for our beliefs is one that we arrive at only after we already believe. In so thinking Pascal shows himself to be a follower of Augustine. Does it follow that, until we have come to believe in God, we can have no good reason to believe in God? Pascal's response to this question is to construct an argument for belief, one that is very different from any of the traditional arguments for the existence of God, such as Anselm's and Aquinas's.

Pascal, in his work on mathematics, was one of the founders of modern probability theory. His friend, the Chevalier de Méré, an outstanding example of amiable and able worldliness, who frequented the gambling tables, asked Pascal to calculate for him the least number of throws of a dice that make it probable that two sixes will turn up. Pascal's answers to this and related questions and the generalizations on which he based his answers led him in correspondence with the mathematician Fermat to construct a calculus of probabilities. He considered the practically rational, worldly person, such as de Méré, to be someone for whom probability, the probability of achieving his own happiness, should be the guide to life. Such a one could not but agree that, if there were a wager in which the difference between winning and losing were the difference between infinite and eternal happiness on the one hand and infinite and eternal pain and suffering on the other, then it is worth staking whatever one has or is upon any chance at all of winning rather than losing. It does not matter how long the odds are, how improbable the outcome on which one wagers, if wagering on that outcome gives one any chance at all of such happiness rather than such pain and suffering. And, Pascal argues, just this is our situation in deciding whether or not to believe in God (*Pensées* 1966, 418).

Wagering on whether or not God exists is something that we cannot avoid doing. For either our way of life will presuppose God's existence or it will presuppose his nonexistence. There is no third way. Where an infinitely happy life is to be won or lost, while what you are staking is finite, "That leaves no choice." Rationality requires that we wager that God exists. To this it may be retorted that, even if Pascal gave us sufficient reasons for believing that it would be better for us, more conducive to our happiness, to believe that God exists, he has given us no reason to believe that, in fact, God exists. And Pascal does not disagree. What he provided us with is a sufficient reason for transforming ourselves into believers. How are we to do this? We are to follow the example of others who have already achieved such a transformations. "They behaved just as if they did believe, taking holy water, having masses said, and so on. That will make you believe quite naturally . . ." (*Pensées* 1966, 418). We are, that is to say, to subject ourselves to a course of psychological conditioning designed to produce belief where formerly there was unbelief.

How seriously are we to take this? If we suppose Pascal to be speaking in his own voice in these passages, then he is giving us psychological advice that is bad advice, as he must surely have known. For it is notorious that conditioning of such a kind is only effective with those who are unaware that they are being subjected to conditioning. Moreover, as Pascal must also have known, it is bad theological advice. For there is no reason to believe that God finds belief arrived at in this way acceptable. The irony is that someone who wagers on God's existence and then conditions himself, so duping himself into believing in God, may find that it is those very actions that prevent him from achieving eternal happiness. So what is Pascal doing in presenting us with these thoughts? What are we to make of Pascal's account of the wager?

We need first to take note of Pascal's intentions in writing what his friends later published as the *Pensées*, a work unfinished at his death. Pascal seems to have intended to cast his thoughts in the form of a dialogue between a devout Christian and a worldly unbeliever and the order that he gave to those thoughts, as he wrote them down, may have been only a provisional order, so that there is much room for scholarly speculation about his intentions in particular passages. What I want to suggest is that perhaps the account of the wager is to be read not as Pascal's view of what is involved in becoming a Christian—about which he tells us a good deal elsewhere—but instead as Pascal's view of how conversion to Christianity must appear from the standpoint of a worldly unbeliever, a view of conversion that is deeply flawed. Pascal's argument would on this interpretation be designed to show that the worldly unbeliever is irrational from his own standpoint in refusing to do whatever he can to become a Christian. Yet in fact the worldly unbeliever cannot arrive at the truth unaided by grace, for only God's grace-conferring action—the kind of action that Pascal had experienced on the night of his conversion—can transform one into a genuine believer. This, however, is not how what Pascal wrote about the wager has been understood by his readers.

I noted earlier that Pascal owed his conception of the Christian life to the pastoral theology of Saint-Cyran, a conception that had been embodied in the rule of life of the convent of Port Royal and of the community of the *Solitaires*, those professional men who had abandoned their worldly careers and devoted themselves to prayer, spiritual reading, and the service of the convent. Saint-Cyran's friend from his student days, Cornelius Jansen, bishop of Ypres, had provided him and them with a definitive statement of their shared theological standpoint in his book, *Augustinus*, published in 1640, two years after Jansen's death. Jansen's formulations of what he took to be Augustine's doctrines seemed to leave no place at all for the exercise of human free will by individuals in either assenting to or refusing the offer of God's grace and this led first to accusations of heresy and finally to a papal condemnation of five propositions said to be asserted and defended in *Augustinus*. At the same time the Jansenists at Port Royal were involved in extended controversies with other Catholics, especially, but not only Jesuits, who had a very different conception of the relationship between Catholic faith and the pursuit of a secular calling. In those multiplying controversies the Jansenists' protagonist was Antoine Arnauld, priest and doctor of theology at the Sorbonne, until he was expelled from its faculty. His oldest sister, Angélique, had, as abbess, been responsible for the reform of the rule of life at Port Royal and for appointing Saint-Cyran as its spiritual director. Arnauld himself also contributed to the life of Port Royal in other ways.

The community at Port Royal had founded its own schools and it was for their pupils that Arnauld designed a logic textbook, although the schools were to be closed down before the textbook was published in 1662. *Logique ou l'art de penser* (*Logic or the Art of Thinking*) was written in collaboration with Arnauld's secretary, Pierre Nicole. It was to become during the next 150 years widely influential and, although its intellectual importance is in some ways independent of the Jansenist theology that it presupposed, it opened up a new way of integrating Catholic faith and secular philosophy.

Aquinas in the thirteenth century, confronted with the physics, metaphysics, psychology, ethics, and politics of Aristotle, had asked how these could be integrated with Augustinian theology. Arnauld in the seventeenth century takes Aristotle's philosophy to have been on central issues decisively defeated in the course of the rise of the new science and the transformation of philosophy. It is Descartes who has now set philosophy on a new path, one concordant with and supportive of the changes in physics and other sciences and, insofar as those who hold the Catholic faith have to concern themselves with philosophical issues, it is from within a Cartesian standpoint and in Cartesian terms that they should do so. It was not that Arnauld agreed with Descartes on every point. He had presented objections to some theses in the *Meditations*. And, unlike Descartes, he believed that skepticism presented no threat and did not need to be answered. How then do Arnauld and Nicole proceed?

What they intend is not a textbook in logic, either as we now understand it or as Aristotle understood it. Their subtitle is apt: they aspire to teach the art of thinking and the aim of that art is to correct our tendency to make false judgments. Sometimes such false judgments are indeed the result of mistaken inferences, and so Arnauld and Nicole do pay some considerable attention to syllogistic rules. But this is not on their view the principal source of human error. Most false judgments "are caused only by impetuosity and lack of attention, which make us judge recklessly about things we know only confusedly and obscurely" (Arnaud 1996, 6). We tend to be either too willing to believe, victims of our own credulity and superstition, or too unwilling to believe, too cynical or skeptical. Arnauld and Nicole agree with Pascal in holding that no one ever is a genuine sceptic. But they go beyond Pascal in leveling moral accusations at skeptics.

Of skeptical views they say "that no one was ever seriously convinced of them. They were games and amusements for idle and clever people. But they were never views that they inwardly endorsed and on which they tried to act. This is why the best way to convince these philosophers is to recall them to their consciences and good faith" (Arnauld 1996, 228). Skepticism is then one kind of moral fault. Credibility, a willingness to be persuaded of absurdities, is another. Underlying both skepticism and credibility is vanity. *Logic or the Art of Thinking*, therefore, has a moral as well as an intellectual purpose. Sound judgment and good character are inseparable. Throughout *Logic or the Art of Thinking*, examples are chosen, so that they are morally and religiously edifying. Compound propositions with more than one attribute are illustrated by "A sound mind hopes for prosperity in adversity and fears adversity in prosperity" (Arnauld 1996, 97), while one example of a disjunctive syllogism cited is "All wicked persons must be punished either in this world or the other. Now there are wicked persons who are not punished in the world. Hence they will be in the other" (Arnauld 1996, 171).

Although the instruction provided by *Logic or the Art of Thinking* enables us to identify those axioms that provide the sciences with their foundations, the study of it is not intended as a prologue to the study of such sciences as geometry, astronomy, and physics, since such sciences "are completely worthless, considered in and for themselves" (Arnauld 1996, 5). The study of the sciences finds its true point and purpose in exercising and perfecting the capacities of the mind. What we have to learn is to be attentive and observant in respect of whatever it is that is presented to the mind, so that about what is thus presented we may judge truly. For true judgment is not a matter of bringing standards derived from elsewhere to bear upon what is presented to our minds. "Just as no other marks are needed to distinguish light from darkness except the light itself which makes itself sensed sufficiently, so no marks are necessary to recognize the truth but the very brightness which surrounds it and to which the mind submits, persuading it in spite of itself" (Arnauld 1996, 8).

What then is presented to the mind? The answer that Arnauld and Nicole give is Descartes's answer: "The simple view we have of things that present themselves to the mind is called *conceiving*, as when we represent to ourselves a sun, an earth, a tree, a circle, a square, thought, and being, without forming any explicit judgment about them. The form by which we represent these things is called an *idea*" (Arnauld 1996, 23). But what it is to have an idea is not further definable. "The word 'idea' is one of those that are so clear that they cannot be explained by others, because none is more clear and simple" (Arnauld 1996, 25).

Conceiving something is to be distinguished from imagining it. We can conceive of a geometrical figure with ten thousand angles, but we cannot imagine such a figure. Failure to make this distinction results in confusions about ideas and about their origins. Arnauld and Nicole deny what Pierre Gassendi had asserted, that all our ideas originate from our sense experience. Among those ideas that do not and cannot so originate are the idea of God and the ideas of thought and being. For, asserted Arnauld and Nicole, "There is nothing we conceive more distinctly than our thought itself, nor any proposition clearer to us than this: 'I think, therefore I am'" (Arnauld 1996, 29). The Cogito is thus invoked, not as an answer to skepticism, but as a paradigm of clarity and distinctness in ideas and clarity and distinctness are marks of truth (Arnauld 1996, 227–28). What is not clear and distinct is confused, and Arnauld and Nicole stress that it is important not to confuse the confused with the obscure. An idea may be obscure without being in the least unclear. Such is the idea of God, the idea of a being who is eternal, omnipotent, all wise, and all good (Arnauld 1996, 27), and who is incorporeal, invisible, and everywhere present (Arnauld 1996, 30).

God is not the only incorporeal, invisible being. When we inspect our ideas, we discover that we have ideas of two different and distinct kinds of substance, substances whose essential properties are those of thought and substances whose essential properties are those of extension, minds and bodies. Such properties as those of "thinking, doubting, remembering, willing, and reasoning" belong to mind. Such properties as those of "extension, shape, mobility, and divisibility" belong to body. Moreover no property that belongs to body also belongs to mind and vice versa (Arnauld 1996, 32). Arnauld and Nicole use the words "mind" and "soul" interchangeably and they argue that, while bodies can be destroyed by change or dissolution of their several parts, the soul, because it "is in no way divisible or composed of parts," "cannot perish, and consequently is immortal" (Arnauld 1996, 237).

By adopting Descartes's view of body and mind or soul Arnauld puts himself at odds with Aristotle and Aquinas. Aristotle's account of substances in terms of form and matter is, say Arnauld and Nicole, not so much false as trivial: "After having learned of those things we seem not to have learned anything new, nor to be in a better position to make sense of any of the effects of nature" (Arnauld 1996, 20). Moreover, when the relationship of soul to body is understood in terms of form and matter, as Aristotle and Aquinas understand it, errors about the soul result. For, when Aristotle defined the soul in the *De Anima*, he did so in such a way that we can and must speak not only of humans, but also of nonhuman animals as having souls. Yet on Arnauld's Cartesian view, he thereby "defined a chimera" (Arnauld 1996, 128), since nonhuman animals lack souls. They belong to the world of bodies, a realm that has its own regular order, events in which are to be explained mechanically. "No body is capable of moving itself" (Arnauld 1996, 250) and "No body can move another body if it is not itself in motion" (Arnauld 1996, 251).

How then are minds or souls related to their human bodies? For both Descartes and Arnauld this presents a problem. Descartes and Arnauld recognize that mind and body do interact. Yet, if they are defined as Descartes and Arnauld define them, it is difficult to understand how such interaction could be possible. How can the immaterial interact with the material? Here, if Descartes and Arnauld are right in understanding mind and body as they do, we seem to have reached one of the limits of human understanding. We also move toward those limits whenever we think about God and about his effects in the material world.

Since matter cannot move itself, the first motion must have been imparted to bodies by God (Arnauld 1996, 166). But God sometimes acts, not through the normal regularities of matter in motion, but by miraculous interventions, by events that do not conform to those regularities. What reasons have we to believe that such events do in fact occur? The only reasons are provided by the testimony of trustworthy individuals to the occurrence of such events. So Arnauld in his otherwise Cartesian catalog of those truths that may be used as axioms, as foundations for our knowledge, includes not only such axioms as "Everything contained in the clear and distinct idea of a thing can be truthfully affirmed of it" (the first) and "No body is capable of moving itself" (the sixth), but also axioms about whose testimony is to be treated as trustworthy.

The first of these concerns God: "The testimony of an infinitely powerful, wise, good, and true person should have more power to persuade the mind than the most convincing reasons" (the tenth axiom). So on matters on which God has spoken to us directly through his self-revelation it is rational to accept what God declares as true, no matter how strong the reasoning to be adduced for believing otherwise. With human beings, of course, it is not so, since "All humans are liars, according to Scripture and it can happen that people who assure us that something is true may themselves be mistaken" (Arnauld 1996, 261). Nonetheless, so Arnauld and Nicole's eleventh axiom declares, on matters of sense experience, where there are a number of individuals with firsthand experience "from different times, different nations, and diverse interests," on whom no suspicion of having conspired together rests, their testimony "should be considered as constant and indubitable as if we had seen them with our own eyes" (Arnauld 1996, 251).

Arnauld and Nicole are careful to distinguish between questions about the occurrence of events, where nothing is at stake except the trustworthiness of human testimony, and questions about the occurrence of events where it is of crucial importance whether or not we have faith in God's word and action. But even in these latter cases we need to exercise our reason in evaluating the credibility of witnesses. So he considers miracles reported by Augustine, including miraculous cures in Italy and in Africa, and concludes on the basis of the testimony of those who were present "that there is no reasonable person who should not recognize the hand of God" (Arnauld 1996, 269).

The importance of whether or not certain alleged particular miracles have or have not occurred concerns for Arnauld and Nicole not only those miracles reported in scripture or in the history of the earlier church, but also those apparently miraculous events that had occurred in and around Port Royal. These were taken by the Jansenists to be signs of God's special favor and the enemies of Port Royal responded by doubting their occurrence. The difficulty for these doubters was that the occurrence of the relevant events was attested by numerous observers. These observers were, it is true, members and friends of the Port Royal community. But since moral rigorism and more especially rigorism about truth and falsehood—on this see Pascal's *Provincial Letters*—were central to the Jansenist way of life, it was difficult to impugn the credibility of those reports. For any sincere Jansenist who was less than scrupulous about the truth believed that she or he thereby risked the eternal pain of hell.

It is not unimportant that, when in the next century David Hume advanced an argument designed to discredit all and any belief in the occurrence of miracles, his argument purports to show that no report of any miracle can be credible, no matter how strong and no matter whose testimony is in its favor. The sheer improbability of such an event outweighs all and any testimony. Hume's dislike of the Catholic religion was at its most intense in his scorn for Pascal and it seems likely that, when he wrote against miracles, he had the miracles at Port Royal particularly in mind. Certainly his argument seems to be aimed directly at the arguments of Arnauld and Nicole.

Arnauld and Nicole by contrast take it that the improbability of an event, no matter how great, cannot outweigh the firsthand testimony of sufficient numbers and kinds of witnesses who are known to be reliable. They also of course hold that it matters, in assessing whether or not an alleged event happened, how probable or improbable it is that in these particular circumstances this type of event should have occurred—and the more improbable the event, the more and better the testimony we need. This holds true of life in general and not just in matters of religion. We are to guide our lives by probability in predicting the outcomes of alternative courses of action between which we have to choose.

Here as elsewhere we have to strike a mean between excessive caution and rashness. Arnauld and Nicole follow Pascal's lead in thinking about the probabilities of outcomes in terms of games of chance and lotteries. There are some bets that we should never make, whether in such games or in life: "Sometimes the success of something is so unlikely that however advantageous it may be, and however little risk there is in obtaining it, it is preferable not to chance it" (Arnauld 1996, 275). So we should proportion our hopes and our fears not only to the greatness of the benefit or harm, but also to the probability of our receiving that benefit or suffering harm.

Yet there are benefits and harms so great that even the slightest chance of gaining or avoiding them is worthwhile. Such are the infinite benefits and harms of salvation and damnation. So "all reasonable people draw this conclusion, with which we will end this *Logic*, that the greatest of all follies is to use one's time and life for something other than what will be useful in acquiring a life that will never end" (Arnauld 1996, 275). This thought with which the *Logic* ends is a characteristically Jansenist thought. Intellectual enquiry, like all other secular pursuits, is taken to have no worth whatsoever in itself, but to be worthwhile *only* as a means to our salvation. Contrast Aquinas, for whom many secular pursuits and, notably, intellectual enquiry are worthwhile in themselves and as such to be offered to God as part of that offering that is the path to our salvation.

Arnauld's Cartesianism was a philosophically daring, but doomed enterprise, just because it identified Catholic Christianity with a dualist view of human nature that is not only philosophically untenable, but also a view that makes it impossible to understand the unity of the human being. Its unfortunate legacy was to reinforce the assumption that we must understand the relationships of soul, mind, and body *either* in materialistic *or* in dualist terms, so obscuring from view the very possibility of a third way, such as Aquinas's.

References

Arnauld, Antoine. *Logic or the Art of Thinking.* Trans. and ed. J. V. Buroker. Cambridge, UK: Cambridge University Press, 1996.

Menn, Stephen. *Descartes and Augustine.* Cambridge, UK: Cambridge University Press, 1998.

Pascal, Blaise. *Pensées.* Trans. A. J. Krailsheimer. London: Penguin Books, 1966.

MODERNITY

~

CHAPTER FIFTEEN

The Catholic Absence From and Return to Philosophy, 1700–1850

Arnauld's addiction to continuing controversy recurrently offended both the Church and the king of France. He was finally forced into exile in the Netherlands, where he continued to defend both his theological and his philosophical positions against all comers. Nicole, who had loyally accompanied him into exile, finally tired of their unsettled and disputatious mode of life, made peace with the authorities, and returned home to France, where he died in 1695. Arnauld died in Brussels the previous year. Among those with whom he latterly disputed was the Oratorian priest and philosopher, Nicolas de Malebranche (1638–1715), who published *The Search for Truth* in 1674.

Malebranche, like Arnauld, followed Descartes in believing that what we, as minds, are directly aware of are *ideas*. But Malebranche conceived of ideas in a significantly different manner from either Descartes or Arnauld, taking our ideas to be not just ours, but ideas that are in the mind of God. In apprehending them we apprehend the world as God sees it, that is, as it is. So the objectivity of our perceptions is guaranteed. Arnauld in his *On True and False Ideas* (1683) attacked Malebranche's account of ideas, defending the conception advanced in *Logic, or the Art of Thinking*, according to which in apprehending an idea, I also apprehend that of which it is an idea, the objective reality presented in and through the idea. Ideas are not representations.

Malebranche, although in many respects a faithful Cartesian, also revised Descartes's views on other matters. Arguing that something can be the cause of something else, only if there is a necessary connection between the two, he argued further that the only true cause is God, since, only if God acts to make something happen, does that something happen necessarily. It follows that no finite and contingent act, event, or state of affairs can be the cause of any other finite and contingent act, event, or state of affairs. In our experience we encounter many regularities such that acts, events, or states of affairs of type A uniformly precede acts, events, or states of affairs of type B, and we develop the habit of taking the former to be the cause of the latter. But this is a mistake, since in such cases there is no necessary connection between what is taken to be a cause and what is taken to be an effect. It is God alone who is the cause both of the former and of the latter and also of their being regularly conjoined in our experience.

By so arguing Malebranche offered a solution to a problem that had appeared insoluble within a strictly Cartesian framework. If mind and body are what Descartes—and Arnauld—believed them to be, it is difficult to understand how it is possible for them to interact causally, how, for example, a decision to stand up could be the cause of movements of the legs. If, however, Malebranche were right, this problem disappears. No mental act, event, or state of affairs is or could be the cause or effect of any bodily act, event, or state of affairs. It is God, the sole cause, who causes the mental act that is the decision to stand up and causes in the next moment the bodily movement. So there is no such thing as mind-body interaction and therefore no problem concerning it.

But the effect of Malebranche's arguments was not to sustain Cartesianism, for Cartesianism was already a lost philosophical cause. Descartes's physics was to be displaced by Newton's. Descartes's metaphysical system gave way to those of Spinoza and Leibniz. Descartes's epistemology could not withstand the challenge of the English, Irish, and Scottish empiricists, the most notable of them, David Hume, who concluded that there is no such thing as causal necessity and that to speak of cause and effect is just to speak of those uniform regularities in our experience to which Malebranche had referred. For A to be the cause of B is no more than for B to be constantly conjoined with A in our experience. So on Hume's account of causality, unlike Malebranche's, there is no place left for God, no function that God is needed to perform. More generally, as modern philosophy moved beyond its Cartesian beginnings, its conception of the nature and limits of human knowledge and of the universe, insofar as it is knowable, leaves no place for the God of theism.

Both Thomist and Scotist philosophy continued to be taught in the universities of Catholic nations and in the houses of study of the Dominican and Franciscan orders. But what was taught to successive generations of

Dominican and Franciscan novices was no more than an arid restatement of older theses and arguments, a kind of teaching well designed to kill any impulse to philosophical questioning. There was in consequence no dialogue between Catholic philosophers and the seminal thinkers in the development of modern philosophy. Where philosophy flourished, Catholic faith was absent. Where the Catholic faith was sustained, philosophy failed to flourish. It was not that there were no notable Catholic thinkers. The Croatian Jesuit, Josip Rudjer Boscovich (1711–1787), was a remarkable mathematician, astronomer, and physicist. But, although his work was widely admired in both Catholic and non-Catholic circles, his thought had no impact on philosophy, Catholic or otherwise.

The first Catholic philosopher to respond seriously and systematically to modern philosophy, as it had developed from Descartes to Kant and beyond, was Antonio Rosmini-Serbati (1797–1855), a priest who developed his theory of knowledge and of the human person through his own private reading and study. What, so he argued, Locke, Hume, and Kant had not understood was, on the one hand, the crucial place that the idea of being has in our knowledge of the world and, on the other, the kind of unity that the human person possesses. Our most fundamental intuition is of being, of being as possessing its objectivity, unity, and intelligibility independently of us as perceivers and thinkers. Our grasp of the idea of being is exhibited in all our judgments, and we encounter being both as perceiving and feeling animals and as conscious and rational agents, bent on understanding. But those two aspects of human beings are aspects of the single human subject, a subject who unifies and directs the different types of activities in which we engage.

Rosmini affirmed that in conceiving adequately of being we form an idea of God and that we are able to argue from the idea that we have of being to the necessity of divine existence. But his arguments seemed to secular critics to lack force, while to some Catholic theologians they seemed to involve an identification of God and being that amounted to pantheism. In 1887, more than thirty years after Rosmini's death, forty propositions taken from his writings were condemned as heretical. Rosmini's defenders have argued that this condemnation rested on a series of misunderstandings. But, whether this is so or not, it should not be allowed to obscure Rosmini's intellectual courage and his recognition of a need to confront the achievements of modern philosophy at a time—the 1830s—when almost no other Catholic thinker was responding to this challenge.

That philosophy of course badly required a response and a response more adequate than Rosmini had been able to supply. For most of the influential thinkers of the eighteenth- and early nineteenth-century Enlightenment were not only non-Catholic, but anti-Catholic. The Church to them represented the forces of reaction and superstition and the beliefs of Catholics, on their view, were unfortunate survivals from those dark ages between the fall of the Roman Empire and the Renaissance, when, so they believed, secular learning had been in decline. Insofar as such learning now flourished it was, by and large, in countries and regions where the intellectual claims of the Catholic faith were seldom advanced and even more seldom heard: Scotland, the Netherlands, Protestant Germany, and England.

The loss was both to the inhabitants of those cultures in which the intellectual and moral claims of the Catholic faith were not heard, let alone understood, and to the intellectual formation of those generations of educated Catholics who had no opportunity to confront and respond to, let alone to learn from the most important critiques of Christian theism. So encounters with Hume and Rousseau, with Diderot and Robespierre, with Feuerbach and Marx and Nietzsche were postponed. Debates set on foot by such thinkers were characteristically debates in which Catholics did not participate until a good deal later. Nor were they present for quite some time when universities once again became institutions central to enquiry and debate.

It was in the latter part of the eighteenth century and especially in the first half of the nineteenth century that in just those countries—and also in post–Revolutionary France—growing public and governmental concerns about education resulted in new forms of university life. Older universities were drastically reformed, new universities were founded, and new types of institutions of higher learning came into being. In Germany Heidelberg was remade and Berlin was founded. In England Oxford was reformed and University College, London, founded. In France under Napoleon the Grandes Écoles came into being—and these are examples from a much longer catalog. These new or renewed institutions at the outset embodied a number of different concepts of the direction that higher learning and higher education should take. But, as they developed, they shared three important characteristics.

First, the study of theology was marginalized or sometimes abandoned altogether. Even when theology was studied, it had become just one more academic discipline. Second, universities were and could not escape being hospitable to an ever-increasing number of new disciplines. To mathematics, physics, and astronomy there were to be added, first, chemistry and geology, and later on, biology. From moral philosophy there emerged the independent enquiries of political economy, later to become economics, the first of the social sciences to claim its place in the curriculum. To the well-established study of ancient classical languages and literatures was added the study of a variety of modern languages and literatures. History, whatever the period or area studied, was defined as a single discipline. The teachers of and scholars in each of these fields claimed an autonomy for their enquiries that freed them from any concern with what was happening in other areas of teaching and learning.

The university thus soon became a place where it is nobody's responsibility to relate what is learned and taught in any one discipline to what is learned and taught in any other. The irrelevance of theology to the secular disciplines is a taken-for-granted dogma. Although philosophers as different as German Hegelians and French positivists attempted to define for their academic colleagues in other disciplines the significance of their various enterprises, such philosophers were largely ignored by those colleagues, and philosophy itself soon took quite other directions. So a third characteristic of modern universities, as they developed through the nineteenth century, was that philosophy, too, became just one more academic discipline, with its own subject matter, its own methods, and its own goals.

Modern universities thus embodied, not only in the content of some of their teaching—especially in philosophy—but also in the principles underlying their curriculum, a set of attitudes deeply at odds with any Catholic view of knowledge and of the world. Where, on a Catholic view, the study of the different aspects of nonhuman nature and human society that provide each of the different secular disciplines with their subject matter is always to be understood as contributing to a knowledge of the whole, the universe, the key to whose unity is found through theological enquiry, the modern university had set out in a direction that led toward the fragmentation of knowledge and understanding, toward a multiplicity of enquiries accompanied by no sense of any underlying unity. And where, on a Catholic view, one central task of philosophy was to exhibit the relationship between a theological understanding of the world and the kinds of understanding provided by the various secular disciplines, in the modern university philosophy, although still acknowledged as a discipline, was generally treated as unimportant except for those who happen to have specifically philosophical interests. Indeed the time would come in the twentieth century when there were some universities where philosophy was no longer taught.

At the same time well-informed Catholics could not but recognize that the modern university was a place of extraordinary intellectual achievement. Even when great discoveries, such as those of Darwin or Mendel, were made outside universities, it was in universities that they were integrated into the relevant body of knowledge and became starting points for further enquiries. In every field of study it was university teachers and researchers who were at the cutting edge of secular enquiry. But from all this Catholics were excluded, sometimes self-excluded, more often excluded by reason of the Protestant or secular character of modern universities.

At the same time throughout the Catholic world there was a growing demand by the laity for education and for higher education, a demand to which the Catholic hierarchy tried to be responsive in a variety of ways. So far as university education was concerned, the first initiative was taken by the Belgian bishops in the years 1834–1835. There had been at Louvain a university of great distinction founded in 1425, where five faculties—theology, canon law, civil law, medicine, and the liberal arts—had attracted students from all over Europe. It had had one of the earliest chairs of poetics, Erasmus had studied there, its theology faculty had published the Louvain Polyglot Bible in 1547, and a hundred years later Descartes had sent a copy of his *Discourse on Method* to Louvain so that it could be discussed there. In the eighteenth century it continued to flourish, but after the French Revolutionary wars had resulted in the imposition of French rule on the Netherlands, the university was abolished in 1797.

After the defeat of Napoleon the restored monarchical government of the Netherlands decreed that there should be, not a Catholic, but a state university at Louvain. But in 1830 Belgium successfully seceded from the Netherlands, and five years later the Belgian bishops were able to replace the state university by a Catholic university, restoring the same five faculties that had existed before 1797. It was a dramatic initiative and, as the nineteenth century progressed, the Université de Louvain flourished in a variety of ways. But it was not yet ready, its leaders did not as yet know how, to react to the intellectual plight of Catholics in a culture of higher education that was so alien and inimical to Catholic thought. That reaction came from elsewhere, from a remarkable and providential event, the response of John Henry Newman to the Irish bishops' project to found a Catholic university in Dublin.

There are two stories to be told about how that event came to be, one about Newman and one about Ireland, and it is at the point at which these two stories intersect that we have the beginnings both of the modern Catholic university and of modern Catholic philosophy. In 1828 John Henry Newman, priest of the Church of England and, for a time, fellow of Oriel College, Oxford, had become vicar of Oxford's university church, St. Mary's. He was remarkable as scholar, as teacher, as preacher. It had been an earlier generation of fellows of Oriel who had led the way in reforming the University of Oxford, so that it provided for its undergraduates an excellent education in Greek and Latin literature, history, and philosophy and in mathematics, provided that they professed the faith of the Church of England. For to be a member of the University of Oxford at that time it was necessary to assent to the Thirty-Nine Articles that defined the dogmatic allegiance of the Church of England.

Newman, as a priest of that church, took himself to be a Catholic priest. Together with a number of other young Anglican clergymen, most notably John Keble—they became known to the outside world as "the Oxford movement"—he contended that the Catholic Church had been fractured by schism into three parts, one Roman Catholic, one Eastern Orthodox, and one the Church of England and its Anglican affiliates. The Church of England had preserved, so they claimed, the apostolic succession, the orders of bishops, priests, and deacons, the sacraments, and the essential doctrines of Catholic Christianity. No one of the three branches of the Catholic Church was uniquely the successor of the early church, the church of the apostles and the fathers. But each had preserved, along with certain errors, the essentials of Catholic Christianity.

A number of obvious difficulties confronted anyone holding the views of the Oxford movement in the 1830s. First, this was not how the overwhelming majority of the Anglican clergy and laity had understood their Christian allegiance ever since the founding of the Church of England by Henry VIII and Elizabeth in the sixteenth century. Moreover, the Thirty-Nine Articles seemed to identify the Church of England as in all essentials a Protestant church, most notably perhaps in their repudiation of the Catholic doctrine of the Mass and of transubstantiation. It was Newman who argued with great subtlety and ingenuity that what seemed to be the case was not, in fact, the case, that the Thirty-Nine Articles could and should be interpreted so that they were at least congruent with Catholic doctrine, even Catholic doctrine concerning the Mass and transubstantiation.

By so arguing Newman brought upon himself immediate ecclesiastical condemnation. But for him this was to be unimportant, for his studies in the history of the early church and in the development of Christian doctrine had gradually convinced him that, in fact, the only true successor of the primitive church, the church of the apostles, was the Roman Catholic Church. So in 1845 he was received into the Church, pursued further theological studies first in England and then in Rome, was ordained priest, and became a member of the Oratorian order. What gave Newman's story a huge interest for many of his educated contemporaries, Catholic and non-Catholic alike, was the extraordinary quality of Newman's mind, character, and intelligence. This was someone of high intellectual powers, of notable integrity, someone well aware of the claims of the Enlightenment, a reader of Hume and Gibbon, someone who understood what was at issue in contemporary philosophical debate, someone with a distinctively modern sensibility and literary style, who, at a time when Catholicism seemed to be intellectually impoverished and unable to come to terms with the claims made in the name of secular reason, had identified himself with the Catholic faith. So the questions for his contemporaries were: What would this identification amount to? What would become of Newman in what was still to him the alien culture of the Catholic Church? The answers to these questions were to be given first by Newman's response to an invitation of the Irish bishops and then by his response to an attack on his integrity by the Protestant apologist, Charles Kingsley. But before we can consider those responses, we need to understand how the Irish bishops came to issue their invitation.

It had been the original intention of the English Protestant rulers of Ireland, after their final conquest of the island in 1691, to deprive the Catholic and Gaelic population of education in order to reduce them to abject dependence. Catholics were barred from universities. No Catholic could found or maintain a school. The rulers of Ireland were to be Protestant and English speaking. If Gaelic culture continued to flourish as it did, it was in key part because of the teaching of itinerant schoolmasters, who in their hedge schools sustained a tradition of teaching in the Irish language and of communicating a knowledge of Latin—more rarely of Greek—and of mathematics to pupils who would otherwise have been deprived. Catholic bishops had been banished from Ireland and only a small number of priests were allowed: the penalty for a bishop or an unregistered priest who was discovered in Ireland was to be hanged, drawn, and quartered. But as the laws directed against the Catholic faith were first relaxed in practice and then repealed, not only did the Church flourish, but as early as 1750 there was some kind of school in every Catholic parish. In 1795 the British government, by then hoping to find in the Catholic bishops an ally against Revolutionary France, not only allowed, but encouraged and subsidized the founding of St. Patrick's College, Maynooth. By 1850 there was a growing Catholic urban middle class and thirty-one Catholic secondary schools. Catholic emancipation opened up the possibility of professional careers for educated young Catholics and demands for new institutions of higher education were pressed upon the bishops by students and parents.

The British government was well aware of this pressure and in 1845 it established by law three Queen's Colleges in Belfast, Cork, and Galway. These were to be secular colleges, open to Catholics and Protestants, both as teachers and as students. No theology would be taught and degrees would be awarded by a separate examining body, the Queen's University of Ireland, founded in 1850. The model that was followed was that provided by University College, London, founded in 1826 as a purely secular institution where no theology was taught. The response of the Irish bishops to the founding of the Queen's Colleges varied. Some were prepared to welcome any increase in educational opportunity for young Catholics. But the more acute understood that secular universities would inevitably become agents of secularization and that in higher education it is likely that, if an institution is professedly non-Catholic it will in practice and effect be anti-Catholic. The bishops, assembled at the Synod of Thurles, therefore condemned the Queen's Colleges and prepared to found a Catholic university that would be under their own authority. But what would it be to found such a university in the 1850s? The bishops themselves were far from clear. It was left to Newman, whom they had invited to become the first rector of their new university, to provide an answer to their question in the lectures he delivered in Dublin, at the invitation of the bishops, in 1852.

That answer has an importance that has long outlasted the university the bishops founded, the Catholic University of Ireland. Both during Newman's tenure as rector from 1854 to 1858 and thereafter those who led that university had to wrestle with almost insuperable difficulties of various kinds, until it was reestablished, in effect refounded, as a Jesuit institution, University College Dublin. Newman's legacy as a university administrator had provided all too little for his successors to build on. With the philosophy that informed his Dublin lectures it was quite otherwise.

The philosophy that informed Newman's thinking about universities was philosophy that he had learned before he became a Catholic. Three aspects of that philosophy were important. First, he was in general an Aristotelian. "While we are men," he was to say in the fifth of his Dublin lectures on *The Idea of a University*, "we cannot help, to a great extent, being Aristotelians. . . . In many subject-matters, to think correctly, is to think like Aristotle; and we are his disciples whether we will or no, even though we may not know it" (Newman 1982, 83). It is his Aristotelianism of course that aligns Newman with Aquinas on many issues, although Newman was in no way a Thomist. But even his knowledge of and allegiance to Aristotle was exceptional for a Catholic thinker at that time. While Newman was studying in Rome, he was told by a Jesuit that "Aristotle is in no favor here—no, not in Rome—nor St. Thomas." Newman asked him "What philosophy they did adopt. He said none. They have no philosophy" (letter to J. D. Dalgairns, quoted in Ward 1921, 1:166–67).

Newman was also exceptional in his knowledge of the British empiricists and especially of Hume. As a schoolboy in a Church of England school he had been introduced to Hume by an Evangelical teacher who wished his students to encounter the strongest arguments advanced on behalf of unbelief.

J. M. Cameron (1962, 238) has argued that Newman was echoing Hume when he concluded, in one of the sermons that he had preached at St. Mary's, that "It is indeed a great question whether atheism is not as philosophically consistent with the phenomena of the physical world, taken by themselves, as the doctrine of a creative and governing Power" (Newman 1997, 194). In a later footnote Newman explained what he had meant by "taken by themselves" as "apart from moral considerations . . . apart from that idea of God which wakes up in the mind under the stimulus of intellectual training" (194). These words point us to a third philosophical influence on Newman, over and above that of Aristotle and Hume, the influence of Joseph Butler's moral philosophy.

Butler, a priest of the Church of England, later to become first bishop of Bristol and then bishop of Durham, had in a series of sermons, preached in the Rolls Chapel and published in 1726, argued that human nature is so constituted that we are able to recognize in ourselves the supreme authority of conscience as a guide to life. We find in ourselves many particular desires directed toward particular objects and particular kinds of object. When we consider which of these desires to satisfy, we find ourselves appealing to two principles by which we make such decisions, on the one hand, a prudent concern for our own self-interest, on the other, a benevolence toward other people. Both of those are grounded in our human nature. It is as undeniable a matter of empirical fact that we are naturally sympathetic to and concerned about the welfare of other people as that we are moved by self-interest. Their happiness matters to us as well as our own. We are quite as apt to act in ways that are inimical to our own happiness as we are to act in ways that are inimical to the happiness of others.

It is also an empirical fact that we do not always act on whichever of our desires happens to be strongest at this or that moment. We are able to stand back from our desires, whether self-interested or benevolent, and to reflect upon them, since "there is a superior principle of reflection or conscience in every man which distinguishes between the internal principles of his heart as well as his external actions, which passes judgment upon himself and them, pronounces determinately some actions to be in themselves just, right, good; others to be in themselves: evil, wrong, unjust" (Butler 1983, 37). Conscience, so understood, has, according to Butler, unconditional authority. We are aware of its authority directly in ourselves and indirectly in other people. We may and often do flout its authority or disguise and distort its declarations. But, if we attend to it, we will be unable not to acknowledge it.

Newman, on reading Butler, found that what Butler described was something of which he was already vividly aware. But he took it that, in listening to the voice of conscience and acknowledging its authority, we are, perhaps at first without realizing it, becoming aware of God. So, in another of his sermons at St. Mary's, he argued that "Conscience is the essential principle and sanction of Religion in the mind. Conscience implies a relation between the soul and a something exterior, and that moreover superior, to itself; a relation to an excellence which it does not possess, and to a tribunal over which it has no power. And since the more closely this inward monitor is respected and followed, the clearer, the more exalted, and the more varied its dictates become, and the standard of excellence is ever outstripping, while it guides, our obedience, a moral conviction is thus at length obtained of the unapproachable nature as well as the supreme authority of That, whatever it is, which is the object of the mind's contemplation" (Newman 1997, 18–19). Here then is Newman's natural theology, one that like Butler's account of conscience, appeals to our awareness of our own inner experience. How then should we respond to Newman's claims?

It might at first seem easy to be dismissive. Freud and others have made us aware of how what we take to be the voice of conscience may be no more than the disguised voice of a parent, especially the father, as heard by the infant and as mediated by the structures of the unconscious. So we need, it seems, not to accord authority to the mandates of conscience, but to put them in question. To treat those mandates as authoritative will be, it appears, to regress to a condition of infantile dependence. But this is perhaps too easy.

Certainly, when reproved by conscience we need to distinguish that, in the judgments of conscience, which is a just and well-deserved reproof from that which is no more than a reiteration of parental voices decked out with an illusory authority. But learning how to make this distinction—often a difficult and stressful task—is part of learning how to attend to conscience. Citing Freud's theory of the superego, or any other such theory, as a sufficient reason for not attending to conscience may turn out to be one way in which we attempt to protect ourselves from the authoritative demands of conscience, one way in which we resist acknowledging the authority of conscience and, if Newman is right, the authority of God.

I referred to Newman's account of how we discern God's presence in the deliverances of conscience as his natural theology. Newman did indeed believe that this kind of awareness of God is natural to human beings, is something that every human being is capable of achieving, if only they focus their attention adequately. But, when we speak of a natural theology, we usually mean a theology whose conclusions, so it is claimed, can be arrived at by rational enquiry. Yet Newman immediately goes on to say that "since the inward law of Conscience brings with it no proof of its truth, and commands attention to it on its own authority, all obedience to it is of the nature of Faith" (1997, 19). What does he mean by this?

Part of what he means is that, if someone questions the authority of conscience, I have no demonstration, no compelling argument, to offer him. All I can invite him to do is to attend more closely. Part of what he means is that, in entrusting myself to the authority of God speaking through conscience, in committing myself now to direct my life by its future mandates, I am always going beyond the evidence that I have so far been afforded. But it is important that, although Newman therefore understands *all* belief in God as requiring faith, he also understands all disbelief in God as also requiring faith. Believer and unbeliever alike must commit themselves in a way and to a degree that cannot be justified by rational argument or by evidence.

It is not only within ourselves that we are able to discern God's providential ordering. We can also become aware of nature as God's work, but only if we bring to our contemplation of nature the reflective awareness of God that we derive from our engagement with conscience. That type of awareness is central to all the great theistic religions, indeed to all religion, even if it is often presented in distorted and even corrupting forms. It is through God's revelation of himself that we are afforded the means of correcting these distortions and of escaping from those corruptions and we find in the shared convictions of theists, Jewish, Catholic, Protestant, Islamic, a morally and theologically adequate conception of the God whom we are most deeply aware of in our inner lives. Lacking that conception we would be unable to understand the kind of unity that the universe, as God's creation, has. All adequate understanding is in the end a theological understanding. It was this conviction that was central to Newman's thinking about the nature of universities and therefore to the lectures that he delivered in Dublin in 1852.

References

Butler, Joseph. *Five Sermons*. Ed. Stephen L. Darwall. Indianapolis, IN: Hackett, 1983.

Cameron, J. M. *The Night Battle*. London: Burns & Oates, 1962.

Newman, John Henry. *Fifteen Sermons Preached Before the University of Oxford Between A.D. 1826 and 1843*. Intro. Mary Katherine Tillman. Notre Dame, IN: University of Notre Dame Press, 1997.

Newman, John Henry. *The Idea of a University, Defined and Illustrated in Nine Discourses Delivered to the Catholics of Dublin in Occasional Lectures and Essays Addressed to the Members of the Catholic University.* Ed. Martin J. Svaglic. Notre Dame, IN: University of Notre Dame Press, 1982.

Ward, Wilfrid. *The Life of John Henry Newman.* Vol. 1. London: Longmans, Green & Co., 1921.

CHAPTER SIXTEEN

~

Newman: God, philosophy, universities

When teaching began at the Catholic University of Ireland in 1854, its faculty included at the rank of lecturer David Dunne, who taught logic and ethics, and Thomas William Allies who was professor of the philosophy of history. But it would be a mistake to suppose that the philosophical content of the Catholic University's teaching amounted to no more than what was taught under those rubrics. John Henry Newman made it clear in his lectures that, if any university was functioning as it should, then philosophical truths, arguments, and insights would be communicated through the teaching of every discipline, as it was presented in its relationship to the other disciplines. In all its teaching what a university aims to achieve for and in its students is "the perfection or virtue of the intellect," and this, says Newman, I have called "philosophy, philosophical knowledge, enlargement of mind or illumination" (1982, 94). So Newman defended as inseparable a particular conception of philosophy and a particular conception of the university.

What is philosophical knowledge knowledge of? It is knowledge of Truth, the truth concerning "all that exists" and the complex relationships between the myriad of particular facts that comprise the universe. It is beyond the power of the human mind to grasp the universe as a whole, even inadequately, except through first understanding the parts, and so we abstract, for our intellectual attention, the different parts of the whole. "These various partial views or abstractions, by means of which the mind looks out upon its object, are called sciences," Newman said in Discourse 3 (1982, 34). Sciences differ from each other in respect either of subject matter or of how they "view or treat" a subject matter. So some sciences treat of the same subject matter as others, but view that subject matter differently. Others may use the same methods, but treat of different subject matters. Others again have partially overlapping subject matters. We move toward a philosophical understanding as we grasp the relationship of each science to the others and the distinctive contributions that each makes to the understanding of the whole.

If we were to study each science in isolation from the others, or if we were to omit one of the major sciences from the curriculum of teaching and learning, we would go seriously astray both in our understanding of the scope and limits of each particular science and in our understanding of the whole, imperfect as that must always be, the project that gives point and purpose to the activities of a university. For, if we subtract any one of the sciences from the curriculum, there is an inevitable tendency for other sciences to trespass on the intellectual territory thus left vacant, to make claims that are not in fact justified or justifiable by the finding of their own discipline. So economists may pretend to a competence on questions of ethics—one of Newman's own examples—or natural scientists to a competence on questions of metaphysics or theology, something that was not uncommon during the twentieth century.

One central task of philosophy then is to understand both what kind of claims can be justified within each particular science and how these claims relate to each other. Every science is by itself incomplete and partial. But since each is indispensable for our understanding of the whole, none is reducible to any other. Each is a representation of some aspect of reality and it is as the mind grasps how each plays its part that the mind advances toward that comprehension of the whole that it is the end of the human mind, by its nature, to achieve. In the progress toward that end the knowledge of God afforded by the science of theology is of crucial importance and so too is the knowledge of ourselves that we achieve. Consider first the knowledge of God.

Newman takes it that we have as little reason to reject the claims of theology to be a science as we have the claims of any other science. "Is not the being of a God reported to us by testimony, handed down by history, inferred by an inductive process, brought home to us by metaphysical necessity, urged on us by the suggestion of our conscience? It is a truth in the natural order, as well as in the supernatural" (1982, 19). The conviction that there is a God informs and is presupposed by the conclusions of all the other sciences. "Admit a God, and you introduce among the subjects of your knowledge, a fact encompassing, closing in upon, absorbing every other fact conceivable. How can we investigate any part of any order of Knowledge, and stop short of that which enters into every order? All true principles run over with it, all phenomena converge to it; it is truly the First and the Last" (1982, 19).

These two sets of claims are closely related. Subtract the knowledge of God from our knowledge, either by denying God's existence or by insisting that we can know nothing of him, and what you have is an assortment of different kinds of knowledge, but no way of relating them to each other. We are condemned to think in terms of the disunity of the sciences. But it is precisely because we are able to find the universe that we inhabit and ourselves within it intelligible, only if and insofar as we presuppose some conceptions of the unity of the sciences, that we cannot but acknowledge that we do possess knowledge of God.

Newman's theses are highly relevant to some later philosophical disputes. It is just because any conception of the ultimate disunity of the sciences is so much at odds with the kind of understanding that we take the sciences to provide that so many philosophers in the last fifty years, taking the truth of atheism for granted, have insisted on the truth of some version of naturalism, according to which the fundamental and unifying science is physics and the truths discovered by the other sciences are what they are only because the truths of physics are what they are. About the claims of such twentieth-century naturalists it needs to be remarked that they rest on unfulfilled promises. No one has yet shown or even come near to showing that—except for the relationship of chemistry to physics—the relationships of the other sciences to physics are what the naturalist takes them to be. Naturalism is, therefore, as clear-sighted naturalists sometimes admit, a matter of dogmatic faith. But in admitting this they confirm Newman's contention that unbelief requires faith just as much as belief in God does.

The pursuit of what in Discourse 5 Newman names "Philosophical or Liberal Knowledge," something that we might perhaps better name "understanding," has its own end internal to it. "Such is the constitution of the human mind that any kind of knowledge, if it really be such, is its own reward. And if this is true of all knowledge, it is true also of that special Philosophy, which I have made to consist in a comprehensive view of truth in all its branches" (1982, 77). The aim of a university education is not to fit students for this or that particular profession or career, to equip them with theory that will later on find useful applications to this or that form of practice. It is to transform their minds, so that the student becomes a different kind of individual, one able to engage fruitfully in conversation and debate, one who has a capacity for exercising judgment, for bringing insights and arguments from a variety of disciplines to bear on particular complex issues. This is the capacity that

Aquinas takes to be the expression of the virtue of prudence. But there is a crucial difference between Newman's account and that of Aquinas.

On Aquinas's view the exercise of the virtue of prudence requires the possession of moral virtues. But in Discourse 7 Newman's view of a university education, even if successful, not only may but often does result not in fostering good moral character, but in a kind of simulacrum of morality. "Knowledge, the discipline by which it is gained, and the tastes which it forms, have a natural tendency to refine the mind, and to give it an indisposition, simply natural, yet real, nay, more than this, a disgust and abhorrence, towards excesses and enormities of evil" (1982, 142). But this disgust and abhorrence are not in themselves genuine moral disgust and abhorrence. They spring from a fastidious self-regard, a wish to be able to think well of oneself. The vices that such a mind abhors are generally real vices, but the abhorrence is not genuine moral abhorrence, is not an expression of or the result of attending to the voice of conscience. Indeed such abhorrence functions so as to make us forgetful of conscience. "Their conscience has become a mere self-respect. When they do wrong, they feel not contrition, of which God is the object, but remorse, and a sense of degradation. They call themselves fools, not sinners" (1982, 146).

It was, on Newman's view, a failure to recognize the difference between genuine morality and this substitute for it that had allowed so many of his contemporaries to believe that education is *the* means to moral improvement. With those contemporaries Newman also disagreed about what a good education is. But in *The Idea of a University* (1982) he is anxious to emphasize that even the best of university educations may result in a peculiarly dangerous form of bad character, that in which the cultivation of the mind, independently of religion, results in an aesthetic distaste for behavior unworthy of such a mind, and this aesthetic distaste masquerades as and is confused with moral revulsion. What then is the remedy? It is to ensure that the university community is attentive to that in the moral teaching of the Catholic Church that makes the distinction between the moral and the aesthetic evident. What that teaching discloses is twofold: both the moral limitations of a university education and the tendency of university communities to disguise those limitations from themselves.

Moral philosophy, as sometimes taught, can itself be one such means of disguise, and Newman identifies Shaftesbury as a moral philosopher who had provided just such a disguise by assimilating moral judgments to judgments of taste, so that "conscience, which intimates a Lawgiver," is "superseded by a moral taste or sentiment, which has no sanction beyond the constitution of our nature" (1982, 152). A very great deal turns therefore on our ability to mark and define the distinction between moral and aesthetic judgment. A condition for distinguishing adequately between these types of judgment is an ability to distinguish between moral and aesthetic experience. Newman was to say more about this in a book written seventeen years after his Dublin lectures, *An Essay in Aid of a Grammar of Assent*.

In the *Grammar of Assent* he was to argue that our assent to propositions is characteristically not the outcome of demonstrative argument. The reasons that we are able to give for holding this or that particular belief—including some of our common and familiar beliefs—generally do not entail the conclusions to which we assent, but support them in a variety of other ways, and in order to move from these reasons to an act of assent we have to exercise a capacity for judgment, what Newman called, not altogether happily, "the illative sense." He also spoke of this capacity in Aristotelian terms as *phronēsis*, insisting however that there are different kinds of phronēsis and that someone whose judgment in one area is almost unerring may be notably lacking in judgment in some other area. One source of such differences is a difference in the kind of experience that such a one may have had in each of the two different areas and the degree to which she or he has been attentive to what is specific to each kind of experience. Where the nature of conscience and with it the distinction between moral and aesthetic experience are concerned, Newman identifies three relevant differences between the moral and the aesthetic.

A "sense of the beautiful and graceful in nature and art" has respect to the whole range of objects, whether persons or not, while the concern of conscience is only with actions, and primarily with one's own actions. Second, aesthetic taste "is its own evidence, appealing to nothing beyond its own sense of the beautiful or the ugly," while conscience reaches out toward a standard beyond itself, to which, even if it only perceives that standard dimly, it aspires to conform. Third, that standard is grasped as carrying with it a sanction, and this because the judgments of conscience are uttered by something higher than the self, "a voice, or the echo of a voice, imperative and constraining," while no such dictate is present elsewhere in our experience (1979, 99). Lack of confusion about these differences is important for two reasons. If we acknowledge what it is that distinguishes conscience from aesthetic taste, not only do we safeguard ourselves from becoming victims of that misunderstanding of morality that is apt to result from even the best of university educations, but we also place ourselves on the threshold of an awareness of the reality of God.

How should we respond to these claims by Newman? Newman himself contended that arguments—outside mathematics and formal logic—do not have compelling force as such, and he therefore spoke of such arguments as probable rather than demonstrative. A probable argument is one that may be found compelling by one individual, but not by another because of the different antecedent background beliefs that each brings to her or his evaluation of that argument. It is these background beliefs—what Newman called "that large outfit of existing thoughts, principles, likings, desires, and hopes, which make me what I am" (quoted in Dulles 2002, 40)—that make us find a particular probable argument compelling or not. So how we respond to an argument may be a test of us and not only of the argument. We have to become the kind of person who is open to just those arguments that directs us toward the truth. And if, because of our character and our antecedent beliefs, we fail to be open to the truth, this failure will determine our philosophical as well as our other stances. But which then are the arguments that direct us toward the truth?

They will be, if Newman's conclusions in *The Idea of a University* are correct, arguments that enable us to integrate our theological understanding of the created universe with the understanding of each of the different aspects of that universe that is afforded by the enquiries of each of the secular disciplines, by Newman's old age an ever-growing multiplicity of independent and wide-ranging enquiries in the natural and social sciences as well as in the humanities. But if Newman had succeeded to some significant degree in defining the tasks confronting Catholic philosophy, it was evident that the philosophical resources for carrying out those tasks had still to be identified. The problem was that far too much of the Catholic philosophical past had been effectively forgotten by Catholics. What was therefore needed was first to remedy their philosophical loss of memory. That remedy was to be supplied by someone who was—an unlikely and rare conjunction—both a pope and a philosopher, Leo XIII.

References

Dulles, Avery Cardinal, SJ, *John Henry Newman*, London: Continuum Books, 2002.

Newman, John Henry. *An Essay in Aid of a Grammar of Assent*. Intro. Nicholas Lash. Notre Dame, IN: University of Notre Dame Press, 1979.

Newman, John Henry. *The Idea of a University, Defined and Illustrated in Nine Discourses Delivered to the Catholics of Dublin in Occasional Lectures and Essays Addressed to the Members of the Catholic University*. Ed. Martin J. Svaglic. Notre Dame, IN: University of Notre Dame Press, 1982.

CHAPTER SEVENTEEN

⁓

From *Aeterni Patris* to *Fides et Ratio*

It had been Leo XIII's predecessor, Pius IX, who had summoned the First Vatican Council to meet in 1869. That Council had laid it down as a truth, belief in which is required by anyone who holds the Catholic faith, that "God, the beginning and end of all things, can be known with certainty from the things that were created through the natural light of human reason" (Dogmatic Constitution *Dei Filius*, chap. 2). In saying this, the Council made it clear in the strongest possible terms that the Catholic faith has philosophical presuppositions and philosophical commitments and that the long history of Catholic philosophy is integral to the history of the church as well as to the history of philosophy. But at the time of the Council's declaration the prevailing philosophical climate was largely hostile to the Catholic faith. John Henry Newman's was an isolated voice, Antonio Rosmini-Serbati's an ineffective one. Yet for some time there had been signs of change, both in Italy and in Germany. The German Jesuit, Joseph Kleutgen, had published a history of philosophy in which from a Thomist point of view he had contrasted the ethos of medieval philosophy with that of modernity. In Italy there were teachers at the Roman College and elsewhere who had introduced recent generations of students to Thomist philosophy and theology. Notable among those students was Gioacchino Pecci, who became Pope Leo XIII in 1878, and in 1879 he made Newman a cardinal and issued the encyclical letter *Aeterni Patris*. In *Aeterni Patris* Leo urged both clergy and laity to address the intellectual needs of the nineteenth century by rediscovering and renewing the philosophy of Aquinas. He did so by advancing five central theses.

First, many of the errors of the nineteenth century are intellectual errors, errors in reasoning. They therefore need to be corrected by reason and more specifically by philosophical argument. What types of error did he have in mind? They would have included not only those social and economic injustices that were denounced in some of his later encyclicals and the mistake of giving too much power to the state, but also Kantian and positivist conclusions that the natural sciences are our only genuine source of knowledge, and positivist and materialist denials that God exists. Such erroneous positions had to be addressed by identifying the philosophical presuppositions of those who defend them and by developing a philosophical critique of those presuppositions. How then is this task to be carried out?

A second thesis is that it cannot be carried out by relying on the philosophical resources provided by post–sixteenth-century philosophy. That philosophy, from all its wide range of varied standpoints, is a source of, rather than a remedy for, characteristically modern errors. Indeed its wide range of varied standpoints is central to what is wrong with it. For, when philosophy separated itself from faith, as it did at the close of the Middle Ages, each philosopher constructed his own philosophical system from his own particular point of view and "it was natural that systems of philosophy multiplied beyond measure, and conclusions differing and clashing one with another arose even about those matters which are most important in human knowledge" (Pope Leo XIII 1979, 17–18). This multiplication of rival and incompatible philosophical positions generated both doubt and error.

We therefore seem to be confronted by a paradox. For on the one hand the encyclical tells us that it is from the standpoint of reason, not that of faith, that we are to proceed. Yet on the other it declares that a root cause of philosophical error is the separation of philosophy from faith. Is the encyclical inconsistent? Not so, if we remember Newman's view that all of us enter upon philosophical argument bringing with us our pre-philosophical convictions and biases. What faith enables us to recognize is the nature and influence of those convictions and biases as sources of error, something to which we are otherwise apt to be blind. As a result we do not realize how difficult it is to become genuinely rational enquirers, to find the right starting point for philosophical enquiry, for we carry with us into our philosophical enquiries unrecognized prejudices and assumptions. Part of the gift of Christian faith is to enable us to identify accurately where the line between faith and reason is to be drawn, something that cannot be done from the standpoint of reason, but only from that of faith. Reason therefore needs Christian faith, if it is to do its own work well. Reason without Christian faith is always reason informed by some other faith, characteristically an unacknowledged faith, one that renders its adherents liable to error.

Where are we to find examples of philosophical enquiry in which reason, instructed by faith, does its own work successfully? We should find them above all in the writings of Thomas Aquinas. So a third thesis of the encyclical identifies sound Catholic philosophy with Thomist philosophy. In its praise of Aquinas the encyclical is eloquent. It recognizes how he drew constructively upon ancient Greek thought, upon the early church fathers, and upon other theological and philosophical sources. It understands that the significance of Aquinas's philosophical enquiries is inseparable from, on the one hand their broad scope and on the other the detail of those enquiries. What it fails to recognize is the extent to which and the ways in which Aquinas developed his thought through a series of philosophical and theological conflicts and that those conflicts continued, indeed developed further, after Aquinas's death. So *Aeterni Patris* woefully misrepresents medieval philosophy by failing to take account of the wide range of rival philosophical positions that were in recurrent contention. This is one major defect in the encyclical, but it does not detract from its fourth thesis, that the time had now come to foster the teaching of Thomist philosophy throughout the Catholic Church.

To this injunction there was a set of remarkable responses of very different kinds. There was first of all—and Leo made this one of his own personal concerns—the scholarly recovery of Aquinas's writings and thought through a return to the manuscript sources and the publication of well-edited texts and both scholarly and philosophical commentaries. There was at the same time a remaking of the content and structure of philosophy courses in Catholic seminaries and colleges and in the upper classes of Catholic high schools. The result was a prodigious output of textbooks, manuals expounding ethics or metaphysics or the philosophy of nature *ad mentem divi Thomae*, and a multiplication of teachers who very soon had themselves been largely trained by reading these textbooks.

Between these two enterprises, on the one hand the scholarly and philosophical recovery of Aquinas's thought in all its subtlety and detail and on the other the propagation of a formulaic, second- or third-hand textbook version of that thought, there was an inevitable tension. Those engaged in the former enterprise were learning how to raise what were for them new questions, with intellectually challenging answers; those engaged in the latter too often learned to be content with stock answers to questions that they did not fully understand. Those both outside and inside the Catholic

Church who were or later came to be dismissive of Thomism had generally failed to distinguish the two enterprises adequately. At its worst textbook Thomism had the effect on those who assimilated it of making them not just insensitive to, but unaware of the questions and concerns of the contemporary secular philosopher, while the Thomism that was genuinely informed by Aquinas's insights became able to engage in a long needed constructive dialogue with secular thought.

In *Aeterni Patris* Leo XIII had looked forward to the possibility of a new relationship between Catholic philosophy and modern science. He was himself deeply interested in the natural sciences, especially perhaps in astronomy. He believed that Thomism possessed just the philosophical resources that were necessary to understand the kind of order and unity in nature that is both presupposed by and revealed by the sciences. This expectation was confirmed by the history of the enquiries that were set on foot by *Aeterni Patris*. At Louvain, for example, Joseph Maréchal SJ (1878–1944) took Immanuel Kant with great seriousness and undertook the project of showing that Kant's transcendental method, if revised to take adequate account of the activity of the intellect in carrying through its transcendental enquiries, as he believed Kant had failed to do, could provide a prologue not, as Kant had thought, to a denial of the possibility of metaphysics, but to a Thomist metaphysics. Maréchal's doctorate had been in the natural sciences and he was deeply in sympathy with Kant's account of those sciences. What he hoped to show was that a Kantian respect for the forms of scientific knowledge presupposed rather than precluded a Thomist understanding of the order of nature and of being itself.

Kantians, however, remained unconvinced and so too did many Thomists. Most notable among those Thomists who were unconvinced by Maréchal was Jacques Maritain (1882–1973), who, like Maréchal, had begun his intellectual career as a natural scientist. While still an undergraduate at the Sorbonne, he had been struck by the contradiction between the aspirations of his scientific teachers, aspirations that he shared, and the view of the world those teachers presented as derived from the sciences. Maritain's teachers were distinguished research scientists with aspirations to make a significant difference in the world. But they presented the findings of their particular sciences as contributions to a nineteenth-century version of a naturalistic and materialist view of nature. According to that view the state of things at any one point in time is no more and no less than the distribution of matter throughout the universe at that time and that distribution is wholly determined by previous distributions of matter and the fundamental laws of physics that govern change. Given how the universe was in the year 500, it could not be other than it was in the year 1000 or the year 1900, when Maritain became a student at the Sorbonne, and it could not be other than it was going to be in the year 2000. The history of nature is a history of predetermined states, holding true of human beings and their actions as certainly as it does of stars and planets.

Yet, if this is true, then what anyone will in the future be and do is already predetermined. Nothing originates with me or anyone else, there is no unpredictability, nothing is otherwise than it would have been, because of my or anyone else's creative decisions or unforeseeable discoveries, and any aspirations that I or anyone else has, as a research scientist or as anything else, to change the course of things, to make a difference in the world, is vain and empty. This, we can infer, is how Maritain must have reasoned in his conversations with his fellow-student, Raïssa Oumansov, who was later to become his wife, both of them convinced that, if this were indeed so, their lives and their projects would lack any meaning. The two therefore decided that, if they were unable by a given date to find sufficient reasons for rejecting the naturalistic and materialistic view of things, they would kill themselves. Happily they found good reason for rejecting naturalism and materialism in Henri Bergson's philosophy.

Bergson had argued that the scientific picture of the world has been arrived at through analysis, a mode of intellectual activity that abstracts and selects certain recurrent aspects of sense experience, so that we become able to master the world around us. Its justification is pragmatic. But what analysis and therefore the natural sciences omit is all that of which we are directly aware, that which we grasp not by analysis, but by immediate empathetic understanding, by what Bergson called intuition. In acts of intuition the mind is aware of itself and of itself as having characteristics that differentiate it sharply from the realities of which the natural sciences speak. Among those characteristics are a freedom, a creativity, and an unpredictability that find expression in the enquiries and discoveries of the natural scientist, but about which the natural scientist, qua natural scientist, can have nothing to say. About fundamental human reality the natural sciences are and must be silent.

In part what Bergson provided for Jacques and Raïssa Maritain was a set of questions, questions to which the defenders of naturalism and materialism were unable to provide satisfactory answers, so rescuing the Maritains from their fear that the case for naturalism and materialism was unanswerable. But Bergson's own answers to these same questions were far from satisfactory and provoked yet further questions. How do those scientific concepts that we form by selection and abstraction relate to the realities from which we select and abstract? When a mind is aware of itself or of another mind, how do the concepts by means of which it gives expression to that awareness relate to the mental realities of which we speak? And what is the relationship between the realm of matter and the realm of the mind? How is human activity, which is at once bodily and intention directed, that is, mind directed, possible? It was some years later before Maritain found a better way of addressing these questions and he did so as a result of his first reading of Aquinas in 1910. It was more than twenty years after that that he published *Les Degrés du Savoir* (*The Degrees of Knowledge*), in which he finally offered his Thomist alternative to both naturalistic and Bergsonian philosophies of science. It is important to note that Maritain's is a philosophy of the sciences, rather than a philosophy of science, and that he focuses upon both the differences and the resemblances between the various sciences.

Of human beings it is true that they are at one and the same time physical objects, composed of fundamental particles, organisms composed of cells, and rational, speaking, thinking, feeling, and willing animals. Physicists, biologists, and psychologists all contribute to our knowledge of ourselves. Each abstracts from the whole certain aspects of it and makes use of concepts that enable them to understand those aspects. The accounts given by biologists are not reducible to those given by physicists, and those given by psychologists are not reducible to those given by biologists. But what each captures through the distinctive abstract concepts that each employs is a reality. What each provides, when successful, are truths and not, as Bergson had suggested, useful fictions, since the mind in perceiving and grasping particular objects and their properties by means of its concepts cannot but recognize these objects as existing independently of and prior to both its perceptions and its understanding. Maritain here appeals to and makes use of Aquinas's conception of truth, and it is also to Aquinas that he appeals in understanding human beings as at once material particulars, located at this or that point in space and time, and yet also capable of a kind of understanding that transcends the limitations of that particularity. This knowledge extends beyond the knowledge of finite beings. So in the latter chapters of *Les Degrés du Savoir* Maritain considers the nature of mystical experience and the kind of knowledge that derives from contemplative prayer.

Les Degrés du Savoir says a first rather than a last word for Thomists. Its principal achievement lies not so much in its own arguments and theses—interesting and valuable as some of these are—as in its project of providing, within a framework constructed from materials provided by Aquinas, an account of each of the sciences that attempts to do justice both to their unity and to their diversity. As such it provides a program for philosophical enquiry, one that remains relevant for contemporary Thomists.

During the first sixty years of the twentieth century Thomism flourished in a variety of forms. The Dominican Réginald Garrigou-Lagrange provided detailed and massive expositions of Aquinas's philosophical positions, presented largely in independence of their historical context. Etienne Gilson, by contrast, undertook an account of Aquinas that situated him in the larger history of medieval philosophy and in so doing was able to draw on the work of a number of historians who in the decades after *Aeterni Patris* had transformed and enriched our knowledge of medieval thought. But Gilson unfortunately and mistakenly concluded that Aquinas's commentaries on Aristotle's texts should be disregarded in identifying his philosophical positions and so presented a curiously un-Aristotelian Aquinas.

Yet other versions of Thomism were elaborated by thinkers who attempted to find some common ground at least with this or that major secular philosopher of the modern period. The result was a variety of contending Thomisms (for an excellent overview of this multiplication from *Aeterni Patris* onward, from a very different point of view from my own, see Gerald A. McCool, SJ, *From Unity to Pluralism: The Internal Evolution of Thomism*). But at the same time a number of Catholic philosophers were developing a range of enquiries very different from and sometimes incompatible with any Thomist stance.

Among these Jacques Chevalier (1882–1962) at Grenoble defended Bergson against Maritain's criticisms and constructed a Catholic philosophy on Bergsonian foundations. Chevalier's student, Emmanuel Mounier, argued that Christianity's gift to philosophy was a conception of the human person that was alien to all major schools of secular philosophy and provided the basis for a distinctive ethics and politics. The Catholic playwright Gabriel Marcel distinguished between problems and mysteries, between those situations in which an appropriate response to puzzlement is to calculate, to construct an argument, and those in which our involvement in some situation is such—in, for example, relationships of love and loyalty, of trust and betrayal—that we cannot but make choices that, if we are open to the truth about ourselves, reveal to us our deepest and sometimes unsuspected allegiances, and enable us to become aware of the metaphysical dimensions of our being. But Chevalier's Christian Bergsonianism—by the end of his life Bergson too had become a Christian—Mounier's personalism, and Marcel's existentialism (it was Marcel who coined the word "existentialism") did not exhaust the varieties of non-Thomist or anti-Thomist Catholic philosophy in this period. Indeed none of them were as philosophically important as two other movements that developed.

At the turn of the century Edmund Husserl (1859–1938) had tried to provide philosophy with a new starting point by posing the questions: What is it that is presented to consciousness in those acts in which the mind directs itself to objects internal to those acts, acts of perception, of judgment, of memory, of will, and the like? What is it that is directly and undeniably given to consciousness? And how do we rid ourselves of those everyday preconceptions and prejudices that stand in the way of giving a true answer to these questions? Husserl's replies to these questions, especially in the two volumes of his *Logical Investigations*, published in 1900 and 1901, provided a charter for a new and remarkable school of philosophy that followed Husserl in giving the name "phenomenology" to its enquiries and findings.

Among the enquiries pursued by early members of the phenomenological movement were some that involved a careful description of what it is to which we are responding in an object or state of affairs when we judge that object or state of affairs to be of value. There was a consensus among some phenomenologists that such responses are fully intelligible only if we recognize that attention to what is of value in such objects and states of affairs and, more especially to what is of value in human persons, directs us beyond them to a transcendent source of value. So they concluded that there is an often unregarded, but ineliminable transcendent dimension to our experience of other persons in their relationship to us. From this starting point some phenomenologists were led to become Catholic Christians, among them Dietrich von Hildebrand, Max Scheler, who was later to reject the Catholic faith, and Edith Stein.

The phenomenological point of view in philosophy is at first sight not only different from, but antagonistic to, Thomism. The initial response of most Thomists, including Maritain, when they first encountered phenomenology, was a curt dismissal of phenomenological claims. For it seemed to them that phenomenologists, because, unlike Aquinas, they begin from a first-person stance, from what is given to each individual's consciousness, will be unable to move beyond consciousness, that they will, like Cartesians and empiricists, be unable to characterize adequately the relationship of the human mind to a world of objects external to it and independent of it. But this was a mistake on their part. For the phenomenologist, in distinguishing acts of perception from acts of memory and both from acts of imagination and acts of desire, not only describes different types of mental acts, but also different types of relationship between each type of act and the objects to which it is directed, including those relationships in which the mind encounters what is external to it and independent of it.

What Thomists should have recognized, and what later on some of them were to recognize, is that the phenomenological enterprise is not mistaken, but incomplete, that its first-person stance needs to be complemented by the third-person stance of the Thomist. It is understandable that they failed to recognize this, since Husserl and most of his immediate followers presented phenomenology as a self-sufficient philosophical enterprise, one that aspired to displace every previous type of philosophical enquiry, including Thomism. But this was not true of all of Husserl's students. Most notably it was not true of Edith Stein.

Stein's earlier philosophical work had been on empathy, on what it is to recognize and to understand what someone else is feeling and thinking. What she showed is that the feelings and thoughts of others do not belong to some hidden inner world of the mind, so that we can only infer to their existence and nature from their outward bodily effects, but that feelings and thoughts are characteristically expressed in and through gestures, facial expressions, and other bodily movements. Our thoughts and feelings are embodied thoughts and feelings. Yet at the same time, since bodily movements thus understood have to be interpreted as expressions of intentional acts of thought and feeling, bodily movements are not just physical movements and are badly misunderstood if treated only as physical movements. So human beings cannot be conceived either as Cartesian dualists, such as Arnauld, conceived them, nor as materialists and physicalists conceive them. Thus by quite another route Stein and other phenomenologists arrived at the same negative conclusions about the mind-body relationship that Aquinas had reached, and this was before Stein or any of her phenomenological colleagues had read a word of Aquinas.

Most of them indeed were never to read a word of Aquinas, but Stein, who was baptized into the Catholic Church on January 1, 1922, and later became a Carmelite sister, engaged in close study both of Aquinas and of Newman, whose letters and diaries she translated into German. In her later work she pursued both Thomist and phenomenological lines of enquiry. Nor was she alone in trying to integrate these two philosophical approaches. In France as early as the 1930s the phenomenological movement had taken on a life of its own, in key part because of Sartre's idiosyncratic development of thoughts drawn from Husserl and Heidegger. But the return to the phenomenological sources that was thereby stimulated led in a number of different directions, one of them toward the Catholic phenomenological philosophy of religion developed in the last part of the twentieth century by Jean-Luc Marion. But that is a story I cannot tell here.

I need instead to take note of another major philosophical movement that had its own significance for Catholic philosophy. Ludwig Wittgenstein (1889–1951) opened up a quite new way of doing philosophy. His earlier work had as its culmination the *Tractatus Logico-Philosophicus* (1921), in which he advanced what he at that time took to be a definitive resolution of the central problems of philosophy. The key to that resolution was an account of the relation between language and the world. Meaningful sentences have a structure that mirrors the structure of the nonlinguistic facts of which sentences speak. Every meaningful sentence is true or false, either representing or failing to represent some state of affairs. But this mirroring relationship between sentences and states of affairs cannot itself be represented in a meaningful sentence. Therefore the sentences that Wittgenstein has to use, if he is to attempt to characterize this relationship, must themselves lack meaning. So Wittgenstein concluded that what he needed to say—or rather to try to say—about that relationship, although it could not be said, could be *shown* through his use of such sentences.

For anyone who accepts the claims of the *Tractatus* the central problems of philosophy, as these have traditionally been understood, will not have been solved, but dissolved. For those problems cannot be expressed in meaningful sentences, although, in understanding what it is that makes the statement of some traditional problems meaningless, we may grasp some deep insight concealed by that statement. So the hope that Wittgenstein expressed in the *Tractatus* was that philosophers, on reading it, would recognize that they did not in fact have the subject matter for their enquiries that they had believed that they had and, liberated from their illusions, would fall silent: "Whereof one cannot speak, thereof one must be silent" (Wittgenstein 1922, 7).

This did not, of course, happen. What did happen almost immediately was that a few philosophers recognized that, if they could show what was mistaken in the argument of the *Tractatus*, if they could correctly diagnose the errors that had generated its paradoxical conclusions, this itself would be a great advance in philosophy. Foremost among that small number was Wittgenstein himself. Wittgenstein took one of his mistakes in the *Tractatus* to be that of having supposed that meaningful uses of language are all of one kind. He took a second mistake to be that of having ignored the range of different linguistic and social contexts that are presupposed by our various uses of language. So Wittgenstein undertook the project of describing in detail the ways in which different types of linguistic expression are put to work and of identifying the range of ways in which philosophical problems and puzzles are generated by misuses of and misunderstandings of language. He asks such questions as "What am I doing when I name something?" and "What am I claiming when I say that I understand what has been said to me?" and "What is the difference between someone's asserting about himself 'I am in pain' and someone's asserting about someone else 'He is in pain'?"

The book in which Wittgenstein presented these and many other enquiries, *Philosophical Investigations*, published posthumously in 1953, had an extraordinary and lasting influence on some major participants in the movement that came to be known as analytic philosophy. Unsurprisingly Wittgenstein's greatest influence was on those who had been closest to him, among whom there were a number of Catholics. The most notable of these, G. E. M. Anscombe, who translated *Philosophical Investigations* from Wittgenstein's German, proceeded to do work of striking importance on issues central to the Catholic philosophical tradition, work informed by her knowledge of Aristotle, Anselm, and Aquinas, as well as by her profound understanding of Wittgenstein. Some of Anscombe's most searching philosophical enquiries were concerned with concepts that are indispensable for the statement of Catholic moral teaching. Consider in this respect some aspects of her account of intention in her aptly named publication *Intention* (1957).

Anscombe had learned from Wittgenstein not to think about the mind as Descartes and Arnauld did, not to suppose that we find out what our intentions are by introspecting and inspecting the contents of our minds. What we need to begin by asking is what part intentions play in constituting our actions as the actions that they are. So someone performing the physical movements necessary to moving a lever may be performing actions as different as opening a valve, testing the lever in order to discover whether or not it is broken, testing his own strength in order to discover whether he can still do what he used to be able to do, and so on. What makes his action one of these rather than another is the description under which he intends his action. Why is this important to Catholic moral doctrine?

If we are to evaluate someone's actions, whether our own or someone else's, we must first identify what precisely it was that that individual did. To identify an action just is to identify the intention or intentions embodied in that action. So we can distinguish an action and those consequences which, by performing that action, the agent intended to bring about from those consequences that were incidentally, but not intentionally, brought about by that action. We do so by considering under what description or descriptions that agent intended that action. An agent who acts with deliberation does so, having in mind the intended consequences of his action, that is, he intends an action that will have just those consequences.

It does not follow that an agent is responsible for all the predictable consequences of her actions. If I intentionally and deliberately do something to which you, predictably, will react unreasonably (I as examiner award the prize to the candidate who deserved it, you as a bad-tempered candidate who failed to win the prize predictably throw a temper tantrum), you and not I are responsible for what is nonetheless a consequence of my action. But if, for example, I intentionally and deliberately do something that involves taking the lives of innocent people, albeit with the further intention of achieving some good through this means, then what I do—the action constituted by and identified through the description informing my intention—is, whatever else it may be, murder. So in evaluating anyone's action the descriptions of that action that are to be considered are all those under which the action was intended by the agent (I take this way of putting it from the foreword to the Italian translation of *Intention* by Mary Geach, Anscombe's daughter, herself a Catholic philosopher of some note). It was as a result of reasoning thus that Anscombe opposed the granting of an honorary degree by Oxford University to President Harry S. Truman, whom she considered the mass murderer of the innocent at Hiroshima and Nagasaki.

Anscombe counted herself an analytic philosopher, taking analytic philosophy to be characterized by its modes of argument and by the types of questions posed, rather than by the holding of any particular philosophical position. So that there was for her no difficulty in being both a Catholic philosopher and an analytic philosopher, any more than there was for her husband, Peter Geach (1919–), as a philosopher of logic and a moral philosopher, or for her student Michael Dummett as a philosopher of logic and language, both of them, like her, among the most distinguished of analytic philosophers. As in the case of phenomenology, we have here a set of Catholic philosophers who, although sometimes influenced by Aquinas and sometimes contributing notably to the study of Aquinas, as Geach has done, are not themselves Thomists.

As a result of this by the mid-twentieth century, or even earlier, the mistake of identifying Catholic philosophy with Thomist philosophy, as Leo XIII seems to have done in *Aeterni Patris*, could no longer be made. So the questions arise: In what, if anything, does the unity of Catholic philosophy consist? Is there such a thing as a Catholic philosophical tradition? If so, what could it be?

Definitive and illuminating answers to those questions were to be given by John Paul II in his encyclical *Fides et Ratio* in 1998. But what made it possible for him to answer them as he did was his earlier training as both philosopher and theologian, in the Jagellonian University in Kraków, Poland, and at the Angelicum in Rome. Poland had a rich philosophical culture between the two World Wars. Positivists, phenomenologists, Thomists, and others engaged in polemical and sometimes fruitful debate. Karol Woityła's earlier university studies, beginning in 1938 when he was eighteen, had been in Polish language and literature. But during the German occupation all universities were closed down, and it was only in 1945 that he was able to return to his studies at the Jagellonian University, now in theology in preparation for the priesthood. In Rome, where he obtained his doctorate in 1948, the director of his thesis was the Dominican Thomist, Réginald Garrigou-Lagrange. To the Thomism he learned from Garrigou-Lagrange he later, on returning to the Jagellonian University once more, added a study of phenomenology, especially the phenomenology of Max Scheler, but he also read more widely, especially in the writings of Martin Buber and Gabriel Marcel. In 1956 Woityła became professor of ethics in the Catholic University of Lublin.

A longstanding project had engaged the philosophers at Lublin, that of integrating phenomenology and Thomism. Although that project was more successful at disclosing the difficulties that have to be overcome, if such an integration is to be achieved, than at overcoming them, Woityła's experience at Lublin extended his awareness of the complexity and variety of Catholic philosophical enterprises in the twentieth century. So how should we now understand the tasks of Catholic philosophy? It was this question that Karol Woityła, the philosopher, and John Paul II, the pope, addressed in a single voice over forty years later, in the 1998 encyclical letter, *Fides et Ratio*.

References

Anscombe, G. E. M. *Intention*. Oxford: Blackwell, 1957.

Maritain, Jacques. *Distinguish to Unite, or, The Degrees of Knowledge*. Trans. Gerald B. Phelan. Notre Dame, IN: University of Notre Dame Press, 1995.

McCool, Gerald A., SJ. *From Unity to Pluralism: The Internal Evolution of Thomism*. New York: Fordham University Press, 1989.

Pope Leo XIII. *On the Restoration of Christian Philosophy: Aeterni Patris, August 4, 1879*. Ed. Daughters of St. Paul. Boston: St. Paul Editions, 1979.

Wittgenstein, Ludwig. *Tractus Logico-Philosophicus*. Trans. C. K. Ogden. London: Kegan Paul, Trench, Trubner & Co., 1922.

～

CHAPTER EIGHTEEN

Fides et Ratio: The Catholic Philosophical Tradition Redefined

Traditions are defined retrospectively. It is only on looking back that the unity of a project to which over considerable stretches of time there have been many different contributors, each with their own goals and concerns, becomes apparent. When it does, it is sometimes because of some challenge to a tradition from outside it, a challenge that awakens in those whose lives and work are informed by that tradition a new awareness, both of their shared inheritance and of the issues and problems that they now have to address, if they are to sustain their tradition in the future. This double awareness is expressed in *Fides et Ratio*, an awareness both of the various strands of the Catholic philosophical tradition and of the challenges to it by a variety of secular thinkers. But it begins with something else, an account of what philosophy is and of the place of philosophy in human life. For it is a central claim made in the encyclical that the Catholic philosophical enterprise is not just one more competing form of philosophical enquiry. It is within the Catholic philosophical enterprise, when it is true to its own highest standards, that philosophy is carried on as it needs to be carried on. What then is philosophy?

Human beings in every culture pose fundamental existential questions about the order of things, about their own nature, and about their place in the order of things. Every religion advances its own answers to those questions, such questions as "Who am I? Where have I come from and where am I going? Why is there evil? What is there after this life?" (Pope John Paul II 1998, 9). Philosophy comes on the scene as the project of addressing such questions systematically and persistently and it does so in the interest of aiming at truth through the exercise of reason. So the preoccupations of philosophers with issues of truth, meaning, and rational justification find their point and purpose in the attempt to answer such existential questions, the asking of which is one of the defining marks of human beings. Because philosophical enquiry is systematic, its outcome has often been the construction of this or that philosophical system, but such systems are never more than partial and imperfect views of the reality about which philosophers enquire. Philosophy is a form of enquiry that is directed toward the discovery and formulation of timeless truths, of the universal principles, both theoretical and practical, of right reason, but such discovery always provokes new questions, so that philosophy perennially has to renew itself, in part by revisiting its history.

When philosophers fail to carry out the tasks of philosophy adequately, it is for the church to identify the need for renewal and to summon philosophers to meet that need. The church thus has a compelling interest in sustaining philosophical enquiry. This may seem surprising. For it is surely an essential part of Catholic faith to believe that God's self-revelation in and through the scriptures and the teaching of the church has provided a decisive answer to those existential questions philosophy addresses. So we might be tempted to conclude that after that divine self-revelation any continuation of philosophical questioning is needless. Yet so to conclude, the encyclical declares, would be an error and this for two reasons. First, reason has its own distinctive way of approaching the mystery of God's existence through its systematic questioning. God's self-revelation to Israel and in Jesus Christ presupposes and does not make redundant this questioning work of philosophy. Second, revelation provokes and elicits new questions by making human beings aware of dimensions of their existence and relationships they had not hitherto recognized, so philosophy is set still further tasks. Philosophical enquiry begins by considering what it would be to understand the order of things rightly and so moves in its enquiries toward affirming the existence of God. But philosophical enquiry finds a second beginning in considering how we need to understand the order of things in the light of God's self-revelation. So philosophy and theology each need and complement the other.

Two aspects of these opening chapters of the encyclical deserve comment. The questions that philosophers ask are, the encyclical declares, questions that they first ask, not qua philosopher, but qua human being, qua plain person. They are the same questions as those asked by other plain persons and every plain person is potentially a philosopher. By asking those questions rigorously and systematically philosophers therefore, we may infer, are to practice their trade, their craft, on behalf of all plain persons. They contribute to the common good by so doing, just as other plain persons, say carpenters or farmers, do. So philosophers owe it to other members of their community to speak and write in such a way that, so far as possible, what they say is accessible to those who are not academic philosophers. The philosopher shares with the plain non-philosophical or pre-philosophical person the need for and the search for *truth*: for the truths of everyday life, for the truths to be discovered by scientific research, for the truth about human goods and about the final human good.

A second notable aspect of this encyclical is that, although it emphasizes the interdependence of philosophy and theology, the extent to which each needs to and can learn from the other, it is uncompromising in its assertion of the autonomy of philosophy as a secular enterprise in its search for truth. Those who exercise the teaching authority of the church have a duty to recall philosophy to its tasks when it neglects them and to draw its attention to errors when it commits them because of their care for the truth, but only philosophers, conducting their enquiries by the standards internal to philosophical enterprise, can carry out those tasks and correct those errors.

The fourth chapter of the encyclical opens with a narrative of the most notable episodes in the history of the relationships between Christian theology and philosophy, from St. Paul onward through the Church Fathers, both Greek and Latin, to Augustine, Anselm, and Aquinas, while its closing sections narrate briefly the drama of the falling apart and the subsequent hostility between theology and philosophy in the modern period. Between these narratives section 43 praises Aquinas for his theological understanding of the relationship of philosophy and theology and points to his conception of and love of truth as the key to that understanding, praise that is reiterated later in the encyclical. For it is not only truth that we need and aspire to, but truth rightly conceived, truth conceived as Aquinas conceived it.

Aquinas's conception of truth is crucial for the overall argument of the encyclical for more than one reason. First, in directing ourselves toward truth we direct ourselves toward God. The kind of concern we have for truth, the ways in which we account the achievement of truth success and defeat in achieving truth failure, cannot be accommodated within any view of human nature that is purely naturalistic. Human beings achieve truth insofar as their judgments as to how things are are determined by how things are rather than by their physical constitution or their psychological makeup. To achieve the goal of perfected understanding a human mind must come to stand in this relationship to each subject matter that it aspires to understand. But it is in achieving a perfected understanding—or as much of a perfected understanding as human beings are capable of—that we understand the relationship of

God to finite beings and become open to the possibility of God's revealing himself to us. Without such understanding we will be unable to give true answers to the existential questions from which our philosophical enquiry began.

The fifth chapter of the encyclical is devoted to explaining why those who exercise the teaching Magisterium in the church must on occasion intervene in philosophical debate and enquiry, in order to draw philosophers' attention to modes of thought that present a threat to their enquiries. In the nineteenth century there were influential philosophical doctrines that presupposed an overestimation of the powers of reason—idealism and positivism both provide examples—so that philosophers tried to supply answers to questions on matters about which only theologians, meditating upon God's self-revelation, can speak. In the twentieth century those philosophers who announced "the end of metaphysics" have underestimated reason's powers, thereby encouraging fideism in theology, a reliance on faith at the expense of reason. It was the achievement of the First Vatican Council to have enunciated as Catholic doctrine an account of reason that both accords to it its proper autonomy and recognizes its limitations. It was the achievement of Leo XIII and of those who followed him in reviving Thomism to recognize that Aquinas's philosophical practice is exemplary in this regard.

How then are philosophy and theology related? Every theology presupposes a set of philosophical positions and it is for this reason that philosophy must find a place in the education of theologians and the education of priests. Philosophy educates the theologian in the nature of the language and the concepts through which the teaching of the faith is articulated and the relationships of that language and those concepts to the philosophical theses and systems from which they are often drawn. Within theology itself a variety of philosophical concepts is put to work, for example, in moral theology. There such concepts as those of "the moral law, conscience, freedom, personal responsibility and guilt . . . are in part defined by philosophical ethics" (chap. 6, § 66).

It is at this point that the encyclical returns to concerns that had been voiced in its opening paragraphs. Philosophical enquiry, like the existential questions that give it its point and purpose, has been from the beginning at home in different cultural contexts. Western philosophy bears the marks of its origins in ancient Greece. But there are also forms of philosophical enquiry that originated in ancient India and ancient China. Theology must engage with each of these. As it does so, we discover in each culture very much the same relationships between theology and philosophy: a movement from theology's starting point—"the word of God revealed in history"—toward a more perfect understanding of that revelation that inescapably draws theologians into conversation with those pursuing the search for truth through philosophical enquiry, so that both theologians and philosophers become aware of possibilities and problems to which otherwise they might have been oblivious.

Yet these conversations in different cultural contexts do take on very different forms. Even within one and the same culture there are apt to be a variety of theological and philosophical enterprises, so different Catholic philosophers have defined their philosophical projects in significantly different ways. The encyclical presents us with a catalog of Catholic philosophical thinkers whose commitment to the conversation between philosophy and theology has issued in exemplary philosophical work. This catalog is interestingly varied. There are patristic names (Gregory of Nazianzen and Augustine), medieval names (Anselm, Bonaventure, and Aquinas), and modern names (Newman, Rosmini, Maritain, Gilson, and Edith Stein). To this list the encyclical adds names drawn from yet another very different cultural context, that of Russian Orthodoxy (Soloviev, Florensky, Chaadev, and Lossky).

What are we to make of this list? Aquinas is there but so are his medieval opponent, Bonaventure, and his modern critic, Florensky. Newman and Rosmini represent very different and to some degree antagonistic positions in the philosophical conflicts of the nineteenth century. Maritain and Gilson were at odds in their interpretation of Aquinas. Edith Stein represents the phenomenology rejected by so many Thomists. Among the Russian thinkers cited there are critics of what they take to be the unfortunate rationalism of the Western Catholic tradition. This list of names is a catalog of deep-cutting disagreements, some of them seemingly irresolvable. What it makes clear is that the summons to participate in the project of Catholic philosophical enquiry is a summons to situate oneself in an ongoing set of conflicts, conflicts that we inherited from an extended history. That history is the history of a tradition. Our present philosophical problems and our present philosophical resources are what they are only because of what they have become in the course of enquiries by and debates among our predecessors, and they are only fully intelligible when they are understood as issuing from that history.

It is, so the list of names makes clear, a history not only of past, but of continuing disagreements. Yet these disagreements have the significance that they have and the form that they do only because they presuppose certain fundamental underlying agreements. When the teaching Magisterium of the church intervenes and condemns this or that philosophical method or point of view, it is because they are taken to endanger those underlying agreements and so threaten to deprive the Catholic philosophical enterprise of its point and purpose. What are those underlying agreements?

They principally concern either the starting point of that enterprise or the nature of that final end, the achievement of which would perfect and complete it. The starting points, as I already emphasized, are from thinkers in different cultures, each posing in their own idioms what are recognizably the same or closely related existential questions. The final end of the Catholic philosophical enterprise is the achievement of an adequate understanding of those realities about which the initial questions were posed. So to uphold any philosophical thesis or argument that denies significance to those initial questions, by asserting or implying that they are either meaningless or unanswerable, would deprive the Catholic philosophical enterprise of its point and purpose. So too would the upholding of any philosophical thesis or argument that is at odds with the conception of the kind of understanding to be achieved and the kind of truth to be attained, if the Catholic philosophical enterprise is to achieve its goals. Hence the papal condemnations of relativism, positivism, and idealism are not arbitrary. For these are all philosophical doctrines that, for those who embrace them, make it impossible either to begin where the Catholic philosophical enterprise begins or to end where those engaged in that enterprise aim and hope to end.

Yet someone may object: Is this not a case of someone outside philosophy dictating conclusions to philosophers? The encyclical claims to recognize the autonomy of philosophy, but surely it makes nonsense of this claim by its insistence on this exercise of the church's teaching authority. To which the answer is: No. It is for philosophers and only for philosophers to judge what the conclusions of their arguments and the outcomes of their enquiries are. But if philosophers seem to have reached conclusions that are incompatible with those presupposed by the Catholic faith, they will thereby have put in question both their faith and the Catholic philosophical enterprise. And if on reflection they affirm those same conclusions, they will have—at least in this respect—separated themselves both from the Catholic faith and from the Catholic philosophical enterprise. It is this that it is the duty of those who exercise the teaching authority of the church to point out to philosophers. They have a duty to do so, just because of their care for the truths of the Catholic faith. It is entirely up to philosophers to determine how they should respond to such declarations, including those of *Fides et Ratio*.

It is not irrelevant that, from the standpoint of Catholic teaching, philosophical reflection and enquiry are activities of crucial importance for human beings in every culture. This puts Catholic teaching seriously at odds with the dominant culture of secularized modernity, for which philosophy is generally understood as just one more specialized form of academic activity, important perhaps for those whose interests incline them toward that sort of thing, but something that has little relevance to practical affairs, something that can safely be ignored by the huge majority of humankind, that is in no way an indispensable part of an adequate education. Yet it is the claim of the church that these attitudes toward philosophy themselves have philosophical presuppositions, presuppositions that, if left unarticulated and uncriticized, make it impossible to think purposefully and rigorously about those existential questions to which the acknowledgement God's self-revelation provides the only adequate response. The tasks that confront Catholics in the face of this cultural challenge are both theological and philosophical. For philosophical enquiry is needed "to clarify the relationship between truth and life, between event and doctrinal truth, and above all between transcendent truth and humanly comprehensible language." So concludes the seventh and last chapter of the encyclical.

What then should the response of Catholic philosophers to *Fides et Ratio* be? How in their terms should they define their present situation, in relation to the conflicts and disagreements within the Catholic tradition, in relation to their conflicts and disagreements with philosophers outside of and antagonistic to the Catholic tradition, and in relation to the cultures that they inhabit? What is it to be a Catholic philosopher now?

Reference

Pope John Paul II. *Fides et Ratio: On the Relationship between Faith and Reason.* Boston: Pauline Books Media, 1998.

~

CHAPTER NINETEEN

Now: universities, philosophy, God

Begin with the milieu in which contemporary academic philosophers are generally at work, that of the research university. The modern research university has been notably successful in at least three ways. The first is—unsurprisingly—in research: in topology and number theory, in particle physics and cosmology, in biochemistry and neurophysiology, in archaeology and history, and in many other areas—the list of discoveries and advances in almost any year is extraordinary. Success in research is the effect of success in producing researchers, enquirers narrowly and intensely focused on solving well-defined problems, on the basis of a knowledge in great depth of their particular limited area of enquiry. The directions taken by research are, however, generally not dictated by researchers, but by those who supply their funding—and what gets funded depends on a variety of intellectual, economic, and political interests.

A second success of the research university is not unrelated to the first. Research universities through their various postgraduate enterprises provide the specialized and professionalized human resources and skills needed in an advanced capitalist society, not only specialized and professionalized research scientists, but also physicians, economists, lawyers, MBAs, engineers, and experts in public relations and advertising. Undergraduate education has by now become largely a prologue to specialization and professionalization, and prestige in providing undergraduate education for the most part attaches to those institutions that prepare their students most effectively for admission to prestigious graduate programs. So the curriculum has increasingly become one composed of an assorted ragbag of disciplines and subdisciplines, each pursued and taught in relative independence of all the others, and achievement within each consists in the formation of the mind of a dedicated specialist.

The third respect in which research universities are notably successful is not unrelated to the first two. Such universities have become richer and richer and richer and at the same time more and more expensive. They have become richer, because they attract massive funding and endowment from governments, from corporations, and from individuals by reason of their place both in the overall economic order and in the lives of students bent upon acquiring those qualities and those qualifications most likely to make them outstandingly successful. They have become more expensive because they charge what their market will bear. Research universities in the early twenty-first century are wonderfully successful business corporations subsidized by tax exemptions and exhibiting all the acquisitive ambitions of such corporations.

What disappears from view in such universities, and what significantly differentiates them from many of their predecessors, is twofold: first, any large sense of and concern for enquiry into the relationships between the disciplines and, second, any conception of the disciplines as each contributing to a single shared enterprise, one whose principal aim is neither to benefit the economy nor to advance the careers of its students, but rather to achieve for teachers and students alike a certain kind of shared understanding. Universities have become, perhaps irremediably, fragmented and partitioned institutions, better renamed "multiversities," as Clark Kerr suggested almost fifty years ago. I remarked of Aquinas, and I could equally well have remarked of Newman, that his conception of the university was informed by his conception of the universe. By contrast the conception of the university presupposed by and embodied in the institutional forms and activities of contemporary research universities is not just one that has nothing much to do with any particular conception of the universe, but one that suggests strongly that there is no such thing as the universe, no whole of which the subject matters studied by the various disciplines are all parts or aspects, but instead just a multifarious set of assorted subject matters.

The contemporary research university is, therefore, by and large a place in which certain questions go unasked or rather, if they are asked, it is only by individuals and in settings such that as few as possible hear them being asked. Yet some of those questions would be provoked by minimal reflection upon the activities of those at work within the disciplinary boundaries that hedge around the enquiries officially recognized by and within research universities. Consider the range of things that are said about human beings from the standpoints of each of the major disciplines.

From the standpoint of physics human beings are composed of fundamental particles interacting in accordance with the probabilistic generalizations of quantum mechanics. From that of chemistry we are the sites of chemical interactions, assemblages of elements and compounds. From that of biology we are multicellular organisms belonging to species each of which has its own evolutionary past. From that of historians we are intelligible only as emerging from long histories of social and economic transformations. From that of economists we are rational profit-maximizing makers of decisions. From that of psychology and sociology we shape and are shaped by our perceptions, our emotions, and our social roles and institutions. And from that of students of literature and the arts it is in the exercise of our various imaginative powers that we exhibit much that is distinctive about human beings. But how do all these relate to each other? In what does the unity of a human being consist? And how should the findings of each of these disciplines contribute to our understanding of ourselves and of our place in nature?

It was to philosophy that in the past the task of formulating and reformulating, of answering and reanswering these questions would have fallen. The assumption made in assigning this task to philosophy was that the practitioners of each of these other disciplines will be unable to understand the full significance of what they are doing and what they are discovering, until and unless they achieve a philosophical understanding of their own discipline and of its relationship to other disciplines. The peculiar contention of theistic philosophers, whether Catholic, Jewish, or Moslem, was that philosophers would be unable to carry out this task, unless they recognized that other disciplines—and philosophy itself—can only be adequately understood in their relationship to theology for two reasons. First, it is only through the relationships of the different parts of and aspects of the universe to God that its unity and intelligibility can be adequately grasped. Second, because the unity of the human being and the nature of human beings also requires a theistic perspective for its full comprehension.

Yet in the contemporary research university neither philosophy nor theology can find their due place. Theology has for the most part been expelled altogether from the research university. Philosophy has been marginalized and in two ways. First it is at best treated as no more than one discipline among all the others, a discipline with no more claim to the attention of students and their teachers than any other discipline has. Insofar as it produces students well prepared for their further careers, it is valued just as every other such discipline is valued. But the notion that human beings *need* philosophy, that philosophy articulates and moves toward answering questions the asking of which is crucial for human flourishing, this notion is wholly alien to the ethos of the research university. And this is not the only way in which philosophy is marginalized.

It is one of the marks of the professionalization and specialization of the disciplines that the practitioners of each discipline are preoccupied with addressing only those within their disciplines rather than anyone outside them and indeed for the most part with addressing only those who are already at work on the detail of the same problems on which they themselves are currently at work. So their mode of writing presupposes not only shared expertise and familiarity with a semitechnical vocabulary, but also a mastery of the relevant professional literature—characteristically for each particular philosophical problem a large and growing literature that has only a few readers—and thereby often enough successfully obscures from view what it is that might give to their elucidations some more general importance. They successfully exclude from the discussion all but their colleagues. Such philosophers inadvertently collaborate with a philosophically uneducated public in making philosophy appear not just difficult—which it is—but inaccessible—which it need not be.

One of the tasks of Catholic philosophers now, therefore, has to be that of following the injunction of John Paul II in *Fides et Ratio* to do philosophy in such a way as to address the deeper human concerns that underline its basic problems, without sacrificing rigor or depth. The need to do so is reinforced by another consideration. On most of the major issues that contemporary academic philosophers address—and it makes little difference whether their philosophical teachers were Wittgenstein, Quine, and Davidson or Husserl, Heidegger, and Derrida—there are currently two or more rival and competing views, giving expression to disagreements that run deep. There appears in almost all such cases to be no signs of any future resolution of such disagreements. Each contending party advances its own arguments, presents its own understanding of the relevant concepts, and responds to criticisms and objections in ways that satisfies its standards, but without providing those who disagree with anything like what they would take to be a sufficient reason for withdrawing from their own positions.

It is not that such discussions do not from time to time make significant progress. The statement of each contending view characteristically becomes more subtle and sophisticated, sometimes more insightful. And thereby it sometimes becomes clearer what conditions *any* worthwhile contending view in this particular area would have to satisfy, something that is a genuine achievement. But even so outside observers who were anxious to learn which of the contending views is true, or at least which has the stronger rational support, would be likely to conclude that it is something other than the philosophical analyses and arguments themselves that determine why particular philosophers take this set of reasons rather than that to have compelling force. It seems that such philosophers must be drawing on some set of pre-philosophical convictions and that it is these that, in the end, predetermine their philosophical conclusions. In suggesting this I am, of course, finding application to the present state of philosophy for observations that Nietzsche made about the dominant philosophers of the eighteenth and nineteenth century. It is worth remarking that academic philosophers in general continue to find it all too easy to ignore Nietzsche's observations.

For Catholic philosophers, of course, a sharp awareness of the relationships between their pre-philosophical convictions, that is, their commitment to the revealed truths of the Catholic faith, and their philosophical enquiries is inescapable. For their Catholic faith itself requires them to have good reasons for assenting to certain truths about the existence and nature of God and to certain truths about natural law. So it requires them to respond to Nietzsche's claim that their uses of philosophical argument and of the conclusions they arrive at by such argument are unrecognized expressions of and masks concealing a resentful will to power. For such a response they need to provide, on the one hand, an account of their philosophical arguments and conclusions that warrants the claim that they have sufficiently good reasons for advancing those arguments and defending those conclusions, and on the other, a justification for claiming a kind of self-knowledge that enables them to distinguish between beliefs and commitments that would not be theirs, if they did not have sufficiently good reasons for making them theirs, and beliefs and commitments that are theirs only because of some nonrational motivation. Concerning what is it that they must give such an account?

The answer is: of what it is to be a human being. At once it is clear that what a moment ago I distinguished as two tasks for the Catholic philosopher are aspects of one and the same task, since any adequate account of what it is to be a human being will explain how and why human beings are capable of the relevant kind of self-knowledge. Such an account will have to integrate what we can learn about the nature and constitution of human beings from physicists, chemists, and biologists, historians, economists, and sociologists, with the kind of understanding of human beings that only theology can afford. What form would such an account take?

It would present human beings—and not just philosophers—as themselves engaged in trying to give just such an account of themselves, as trying to understand what it is that they are doing in trying to achieve understanding, a kind of understanding that will enable us to distinguish what it is worth caring about a very great deal from what it is worth caring about a good deal less, and both from what is not worth caring about at all. So there is a crucial relationship between metaphysics and ethics. For it is only insofar as we understand the universe, including ourselves, as dependent on God for our existence that we are also able to understand ourselves as directed toward God and what our directedness toward God requires of us by way of caring. The philosophical resources we have for constructing such an account are the resources provided by the history of the Catholic philosophical tradition, which is to say that such an account would have to emerge from the dialogues internal to that tradition, from those debates and disagreements within that tradition that, as we have learned from *Fides et Ratio*, are constitutive of it.

It would be a Thomistic account in its overall understanding of truth and of our relationship to God as both first and final cause, but it would need to integrate into its detailed treatments of such topics as the limits of scientific explanation, the body-soul-mind relationship, the acquisition of self-knowledge and the overcoming of self-deception, and the social dimensions of human activity and enquiry, insights, analyses, and arguments drawn from Catholic thinkers as various as Anselm and Scotus, Suarez and Pascal, Stein and Marcel and Anscombe, and indeed from such seminal non-Catholic thinkers as Kierkegaard, Husserl, and Wittgenstein. The theology that it would presuppose would be Augustinian, just because such is the theology that has been presupposed, by and large, by the whole Catholic philosophical tradition.

If such an account were to accomplish its philosophical purposes, it would have to confront and overcome more than one kind of difficulty. It would have to enable Catholic philosophers to engage with the contentions of the whole range of contemporary major philosophical positions incompatible with and antagonistic to the Catholic faith, including the whole range of versions of naturalism, reductive and nonreductive, the Heideggerian and post-Heideggerian romantic rejections of the ontology presupposed by the Catholic faith, pragmatist reconceptions and postmodern rejections of truth, and that so often taken for granted thin desiccated Neokantianism that is so fashionable in contemporary philosophy. To have to reckon with all of these *now* is part of the price that Catholic thought has to pay for its absence from the philosophical scene during those periods in which these secularizing modes of thought were first developed.

In each case what has to be identified is what it is about human beings that this or that particular philosophical standpoint is obliged to omit or to distort or to trivialize or to conceal. In each case that omission, distortion, trivialization, or concealment will be closely connected to some genuine insights, some set of truths, insistence on which has mistakenly seemed to require this or that misunderstanding of human nature. So for one type of view the natural scientific understanding of human beings will have been given too much importance, for another too little. For one the possibilities of metaphysical enquiry will have been exaggerated, for another badly underestimated. And so on. But in every case what has gone wrong will have resulted from some inability or refusal to understand human beings as directed toward God, both in their practical and in their theoretical enquiries. But to this there will surely be objections and protests.

For it must seem that what I have proposed is an absurdly ambitious program of philosophical work. Yet it is to the point at which just such a program of work is needed that we have been brought by the history of the Catholic philosophical tradition. It is on whether and how far some program of this kind can be adequately spelled out and implemented that the future of that tradition depends, and this even though the prospects of success also appear unpromising for quite another type of reason. Because what is required of us is dialogue and debate, both within the tradition and between the protagonists of the tradition and those with whom we are in philosophical disagreement, what we are committed to is a large cooperative venture. Because of the integrative function of philosophy in the Catholic tradition, because of the way in which philosophy has to open up and illuminate relationships between theology and the whole range of the secular disciplines, philosophical enquiry cannot be pursued in isolation from enquiry in those other disciplines. For both reasons its projects require the setting of a university. But the structures of the contemporary research university are, as we have seen, deeply inimical to such projects. So that any Catholic university in which such projects were to be successfully pursued would need to have structures and goals very different from those of the great secular research universities, and not just by reason of the central place given to the study of theology. Both its undergraduate and its graduate studies, especially in philosophy, but also more generally, would be very different.

Yet what in fact we find is that the most prestigious Catholic universities often mimic the structures and goals of the most prestigious secular universities and do so with little sense of something having gone seriously amiss. To the extent that this is so, the institutional prospects for the future history of the Catholic philosophical tradition are not encouraging, quite apart from the daunting character of its intellectual needs and ambitions. Yet a moment of reflection on the past history of that tradition is enough to remind us: it rarely, if ever, was otherwise—not for Anselm or Abelard, not for Aquinas, not for Vitoria and Suarez, certainly not for Newman. Augustine is always there to remind us how finitude and sinfulness issue in the fragility of all our projects, including this one. Like them we can take courage from the thought that, in the life of the mind as elsewhere, there is always more to hope for than we can reasonably expect.

Index

awareness, 23, 24; as thing, 80; unity of, 23, 24
Soviet Union, 16
Spain, 58, 107
species, 36, 74
Spinoza, Baruch, 132
Stein, Edith, 158, 169, 178; and empathy, 159; and mind-body relationship, 159
St. John, 22
Stoicism, 63
St. Patrick's College, Maynooth, 138
St. Paul, 167
Suárez, Francisco, 178, 180; on individuals, 109; as influential, 108
substance, 22, 124
Sufi, 49
Summa contra Gentiles (Aquinas), 74
Summa Theologiae (Aquinas), 92, 97, 106
superego, 141
supreme good: and truth, 32; and virtue, 30, 31
symbolic theology, 37
Synod of Thurles, 139

Tahafut Al-falāsifa (The Incoherence of the Philosophers) (al-Ghazālī), 48, 50; doctrines in, 49
Tahāfut al-tahāfut (The Incoherence of the Incoherence) (ibn Rushd), 50
theism, 8, 14; nature of, 15. See also theists
theists, 142; v. atheists, 76, 77; atheists, disagreement with, 47; and God's existence, 38, 47; human beings, unique position of, 77, 78; and Marxism, 16. See also theism
Theodoric, 34, 35
theology, 17, 61, 67, 94, 146, 177; and education, 62; fideism in, 168; and liberal arts, 62; and philosophy, 29, 30, 68, 74, 75, 166–69, 175; and

secular knowledge, 66; as specialized, 16; study of, as marginalized, 134, 135
Thierry of Chartres, 62
thinking: art of, 123; kinds of, 87
Thirty-Nine Articles, 136; and Catholic doctrine, 137
Thomism, 100, 108, 109, 132, 159, 168; flourishing of, 157; and phenomenology, 158; varieties of, 157, 158
thought: and body, 81
Toledo (Spain), 58
Topics (Aristotle), 34, 51
Torah, 55, 56
Tractatus Logico-Philosophicus (Wittgenstein), 160
traditions, 165
translation: as collective enterprise, 58–59
Trinity, 22
Truman, Harry S., 111, 113, 115, 116; and Averroistic view, 67, 68; and demonstrative argument, 54; and happiness, 25; knowledge of, 145; and philosophy, 166, 167; as revealed, 54; and supreme good, 32; and understanding, 68, 69

understanding, 68, 69, 178
universals, 101
universities, 142; aim of, 147; in America, 15, 16; and Aquinas, 94, 95; beginnings of, 64, 65, 68; Catholics, exclusion from, 136; Catholic worldview, at odds with, 135; concept of, 65; curriculum of, 101; curriculum, as Godless, 17; disciplines, as autonomous, 15, 16; disciplines, institutional form of, 66; enforced conformity, as places of, 105–6; enquiry, as institutions of, 134; instruction, student demand

About the Author

Alasdair MacIntyre teaches philosophy at the University of Notre Dame. He has previously taught at a number of British and American universities. He is the author of *After Virtue* and *Edith Stein: A Philosophical Prologue 1913-22.*